Strategic Planning
for School Leaders

Strategic Planning for School Leaders

Dr. Pamela A. Lemoine,
Dr. Delaine Dupree Bennett,
Dr. Evan G. Mense,
and Dr. Michael D. Richardson

cognella®

SAN DIEGO

Bassim Hamadeh, CEO and Publisher
Amy Smith, Senior Project Editor
Jess Estrella, Senior Graphic Designer
Stephanie Kohl, Licensing Associate
Natalie Piccotti, Director of Marketing
Kassie Graves, Senior Vice President of Editorial
Jamie Giganti, Director of Academic Publishing

3970 Sorrento Valley Blvd., Ste. 500, San Diego, CA 92121

BRIEF CONTENTS

DETAILED CONTENTS

Preface

School leaders need planning skills, now more than ever. The purpose of this book is to assist school leader candidates in acquiring knowledge about practices needed to establish and lead a systemic process, strategic planning. School leaders working with the strategic planning process use all leadership elements: visionary leadership, curriculum leadership, managerial leadership, cultural leadership, ethical leadership, and political leadership. Strategic planning needs to be an integrally functioning educational process; school leaders need to understand what it is and how to provide the leadership elements needed.

PURPOSE

Strategic planning matters. One of the most important roles of a school leader is planning. Higher education institutions teach what educational leaders need to know to run a school; however, few programs provide a base of knowledge in systemic planning processes such as strategic planning. However, a knowledge base is necessary for school leaders who are tasked with planning, designing, implementing, and evaluating continuous school improvement.

School leaders spend a great deal of time on planning; most legislative actions that address school improvement *require* school leaders to be actively involved in planning to improve school achievement. Thus, it is important to increase the ability of school leader candidates to understand how and why stakeholders should be involved in strategic planning, including implementing procedures for gathering and assimilating data for the planning process, analyzing the data, making strategic decisions, implementing processes, and finally evaluating the plan.

ORGANIZATION OF THE TEXT

The order of the chapters outlines the strategic planning process as it progresses in a school setting.

Chapter 1 addresses the first component of strategic planning: what strategic planning is and the background of strategic planning. This chapter provides information about the strategic planning process in educational settings. Additionally, the chapter provides information about the continuous school improvement mandate tied to the Every Student Succeeds Act (ESSA), requirements for stakeholder involvement.

Chapter 2 focuses on another component of strategic planning: the needs assessment. The chapter includes information about ESSA guidance, who needs to be involved in needs assessments, and why needs assessments should include representative membership from all educational stakeholders.

Chapter 3 examines analyzing needs assessment data. This chapter has information about what data should be included in gathering needs assessment information as well as how to analyze, organize, and present data to stakeholders.

Chapter 4 explores developing and prioritizing goals and objectives. Information in the chapter is focused on defining goals, establishing goals, as well as the process of sense making and prioritization of goals.

Chapter 5 is centered on choosing strategies to reach goals and objectives. One of the key processes of working with strategic planning is the need to use the deliberative process of decision making, which must look at not only short-term and long-term practices but also must consider ultimate outcomes.

Chapter 6 addresses building capacity. Building pedagogical abilities of those working with the strategic planning process is an integral process in strategic planning; there is a continuous need to build instructional abilities of those who are working and teaching students.

Chapter 7 focuses on implementation. This chapter defines the processes of execution of a strategic plan as well as the stages of the implementation. The strategic planning process builds to the implementation process through the initial stages with the goal of operationalizing the strategic planning results.

Chapter 8 addresses monitoring, assessing, and evaluating the implementation process. The chapter presents information about monitoring processes as well as monitoring tools and procedures.

Chapter 9 explores ongoing evaluation. With the process of continuous school improvement, ongoing evaluation processes do not stop. A process for evaluation of short- and long-term goals needs to be established to assure that the implementation processes are meeting predetermined targets.

Chapter 10 returns to the cyclical process of strategic planning. When a strategic planning cycle is concluding, the process is iterative, beginning again, based on outcomes from a final evaluation process. Addressing the evaluative results reinitiates the cycle of strategic planning.

FEATURES

The text includes practical illustrations of the strategic planning process that will help school leader candidates work with strategic planning systemic procedures. Each chapter opens with a section entitled "Vignette," a short leadership illustration based on the experiences of the authors of the text, who were school leaders working in the continuous school improvement process. The vignette is a narrative account of the experiences of the leaders in working with strategic planning.

There is also a section at the end of the chapter, "Follow-Up on the Vignette," provides insight about the outcomes for the leader who has been working with the strategic planning process. The follow-up process reflects some of the thoughts of the leader at the end of a school day, reflecting on the challenges of school leadership work with strategic planning.

The "Reflection" section is an analysis and objective piece based on the experience of the authors who worked as teachers, leaders, and district leaders. The aim of the reflection was to consider objectively what was portrayed in the Vignette and Follow-Up on the Vignette in terms of the role of school leaders and their decision-making processes and experiences.

Each chapter has *student learning outcomes* as well as a short list of *key terms*. There is a list of references and bibliographic references.

Resources also include PowerPoint slides available for use with each chapter, and some chapters provide Web links for further resources.

AUDIENCE

The targeted audience for the book is school leadership candidates. The National Educational Leadership Preparation (NELP) standards and the Professional Standards for Educational Leadership (PSEL) provide a list of standards portraying what school leadership candidates should know. The skills are listed in differing standards; however, the school leadership candidate needs to understand how to initiate and follow through with a systemic process, strategically planning how to improve student achievement. This process is required in the legislation outlined by the Every Student Succeeds Act (ESSA). School leader candidates need to have background knowledge about systemic, strategic planning processes, what strategic planning is, and how the pieces fit together in order to provide the leadership necessary to improve student achievement.

ACKNOWLEDGMENTS

The authors of the text wish to express their appreciation to all the people who have contributed to the writing and publication of this work.

What Is Strategic Planning?

Anne Smith is ending her first year as principal after having served as assistant principal of the same high school for 3 years. The school and the district have functioned at a level acceptable to the community and have maintained state and regional accreditation. However, the new superintendent moved very quickly to address some areas of weaknesses that he perceived in the school system. One of these is developing a strategic plan for the district. When Anne was interviewed for the principalship last year, the superintendent indicated that he wanted to implement strategic planning after spending some time getting to know the district. Now, he wants to spend 2 weeks during the summer working on strategic planning and wants all principals involved. The superintendent has appointed Anne as the chair of the principal's committee that will undertake a strategic planning process and will submit recommendations for a district strategic plan. The superintendent did not provide guidelines about strategic planning but left no doubt about his expectations for the committee to develop a district strategic plan to implement this academic year.

Anne has a dilemma; she wants to help but does not feel prepared to address and lead a strategic planning committee of principals. She recognizes her lack of knowledge and experience will not be helpful to the committee; however, she does not want to be perceived as shirking her duty to her colleagues, the district, and the new superintendent. Although she reluctantly accepts the appointment,

1

she is left with major questions: What is a strategic plan? What processes should be used to develop a strategic plan? Where can she find accurate information about strategic planning, and how is it used in other places?

LEARNING OUTCOMES

After reading this chapter, the learner should be able to do the following:

1. Describe strategic planning processes
2. Explain the necessity for continuous school improvement
3. Define the key words
4. Demonstrate knowledge and understanding about the use of a strategic planning process in educational settings
5. Discuss the role of strategic planning in relationship to other administrative responsibilities
6. Articulate a broad understanding of planning skills needed by successful educational leaders

KEY WORDS

Strategic planning

Continuous school improvement

No Child Left Behind

Every Student Succeeds Act

Elementary and Secondary Education Act

Systematic planning processes

Stakeholder(s)

Mission

Vision

INTRODUCTION

School leaders deal with new, ever-changing requirements: accountability in new forms, changing population demographics, decreasing budgets, and requirements to address the myriad needs of students. Addressing what exists and what needs to change necessitates planning; plans that build strength, flexibility, and sustainability for schools also build adaptability and capacity. The ability of educators to plan and to address the needs of students within an increasingly complex and dynamic educational environment requires the ability to develop a course of action using a planning process.

Strategic planning is a systemic process utilized by school systems and schools to set goals, determine the appropriate actions in order to achieve those goals, and assemble the necessary resources to implement the actions needed to reach goals. The actual term "strategy" is derived from the Greek term *strategos*, translated literally as "general of the army." In 490 BC, ancient Greek tribal warriors elected a *strategos* to head their regiment. The chief role of the *strategoi* was to provide strategic advice to the ruler of the tribe. The *strategos* provided military advice regarding how to develop battle strategies (Beach & Lindahl, 2015).

In modern times, management theorist Henri Fayol (1841–1925) included strategic planning as one of the prime responsibilities of organizational management: planning, organizing, command, coordination, and control. Strategic planning in multiple iterations has been used in business and higher education. Strategic planning is a systematic and cyclical planning process that refines the mission (purpose) and vision (direction) of an educational organization; uses data collected in a needs assessment to establish goals, objectives, and strategies; and evaluates continuously to assess whether goals and objectives were met. The process of strategic planning includes an articulation of the guiding principles under which the organization will operate by revisiting what exists as well as what should exist. Strategic planning processes involve making decisions based on data gathered during the strategic planning processes and considering strategies to achieve goals and objectives.

SCHOOL-BASED STRATEGIC PLANNING

Beach and Lindahl (2015) stated that school systems have been using strategic planning processes since the 1980s. According to the authors, most school districts were using some type of strategic planning, adopting the processes to meet educational needs. The Balanced Scorecard Institute (Rohm, 2008) reported that a strategic planning process provides methods to develop fundamental decision-making processes for schools. Beach and Lindahl (2007) also observed that the use of strategic planning in education declined in the 2000s with the implementation of policies that forced building principals to become de facto school improvement planners, usually in terms of addressing **continuous school improvement** mandates established in **No Child Left Behind** (2001) legislation.

With No Child Left Behind (NCLB), planning was reactive and based on mandated results established for targeted groups of students. School improvement plans were based on compliance with federal mandates to quickly improve performance before the next assessment cycle. State and system leaders pushed NCLB responsibilities to school leaders who then presented student achievement targets to teacher committees whose jobs were to plan to remedy areas of academic weakness to improve performance on forthcoming yearly state summative assessments. Leaders and teachers and parents voiced concern that educational performance was strictly based on student achievement scores on yearly mandated state assessments.

The passage of the **Elementary and Secondary Education Act (ESEA)** in 1965 established requirements to improve academic achievement in order to provide a quality education for all children. ESEA has been reauthorized eight times; each time legislation changed achievement requirements. No Child Left Behind (2001), another ESEA reauthorization, added further requirements for annual state testing in targeted grade levels, accountability for student and school performance, and continuous school improvement measures, coupled with federal oversight to ensure regulations were followed and, for the first time, established punitive measures for lack of improvement.

In 2015, the Elementary and Secondary Education Act was reauthorized and renamed the **Every Student Succeeds Act (ESSA).** Oversight moved from federal to state, district, and schools, placing more decision-making powers about accountability and continuous improvement processes at state, district, and local levels. However, with those decision-making powers came responsibilities for districts and schools to assume further commitments to determine what was necessary to improve student achievement as well as legislative language that stated the requirement to adopt systematic processes to improve.

The Every Student Succeeds Act (2015) tied systemic planning in terms of continuous school improvement to requirements for districts and schools. ESSA legislation was crafted with great specificity about requirements for a **systematic planning process**, critically detailing **stakeholder** involvement as a key process for improved student achievement. Stakeholders, according to ESSA legislation, included

> teachers; principals; school leaders; paraprofessionals; specialized instructional support personnel; representatives from charter school leaders and private school; community-based and civil rights organization representatives; representatives of students with disabilities; representatives of English learners; representatives of historically underserved students; representatives from higher education institutions; employers; early childhood educators; and members of the public. (ESSA, 2015)

Guidance from the North Carolina Department of Public Instruction (2016) suggested continuous improvement processes were akin to establishing a "road map that sets out the changes a school needs to make to improve the level of student achievement, and shows how and when these changes will be made" (p. 18). Without concrete, well thought–out and organized planning and implementation processes, schools may lose direction.

While some school leaders and faculties were knowledgeable about how to assess, initiate, implement, and evaluate school improvement plans and strategies, often school-based solutions to improving students' academic performance were based on buying readily available commercial programs to use for professional development, though they were not designed to meet individual school and student needs. At the same time, school-based leaders were overwhelmed with the operation and management of schools, while concurrently juggling school improvement processes required in order to follow financial compliance obligations associated with Title I funding (Eacott, 2008).

ADDRESSING COMPLEX AND EVOLVING DEMANDS

Today's schools and school systems need to be able to respond to complex and evolving demands. Teachers, parents, students, and community stakeholders want to be educationally involved. Educators face myriad challenges: economic competition from charter and virtual schools; demographic changes in their environment; political demands for student performance to improve; societal expectations for social justice movements; technological infrastructure issues; availability and retention of qualified teachers; professional development needs; and continuous requirements and changing legislation at the state and national level, all of which demand continuous school improvement.

THE NEED FOR STRATEGIC PLANNING

The failure of federally dictated school reform efforts, such as No Child Left Behind (2002), suggested the necessity to use systemic planning processes for states and districts and schools as methods to effectively meet the needs of the students, improve educational processes, and increase the likelihood of successful academic achievement. Based on the transfer of responsibility from federal mandates to local level decision-making processes, ESSA guidance promoted the need for strategic planning, a systemic planning process that encouraged schools to develop their own **mission** (purpose); **vision** (direction); needs assessment (improvement focus); strategies (actions to reach improvement goals); processes (to implement strategies); monitoring (accountability); and evaluation (accountability and performance indicators). One key change was ESSA language, which mandated stakeholder involvement in the process of systematic planning.

INTENTIONAL PLANNING

Under No Child Left Behind, when schools submitted individual school improvement plans, system and school leaders rarely spent time considering a broader picture for improving student achievement. School improvement plans in many cases were dictated as school-based plans, guided by Title I and II funding, which necessitated schools in districts to quickly obligate federal monies, justified by targeted performance goals established by federal legislative requirements.

Individual school improvement plans under NCLB were tied financial commitments necessary to put school improvement strategies in place. Because the planning process was tied to assessment outcomes and, subsequently, improvement mandates, schools were hampered by data usually received at the end of the academic year or in the summer after the school year ended. Time for assessing, planning, implementation, and evaluation was tethered to testing timeframes—from one testing cycle to the next and not under the control of local systems and schools.

The Every Child Succeeds Act (2015) added a systemic planning process to be used in addressing school improvement needs:

> A schoolwide program shall be based on a comprehensive needs assessment of the entire school that takes into account information on the academic achievement of children in relation to the challenging State academic standards, particularly the needs of those children who are failing, or are at-risk of failing, to meet the challenging State academic standards and any other factors as determined by the local educational agency. (ESSA Section 1114[b][6])

With school building–level leaders still the responsible persons for overall school improvement planning at the building level, including all stakeholders in education is critical. Harnack and Seebaum (2017) suggest, "Managing a public school district today has ... become a labyrinth of elaborate endeavors" (p. 1), suggesting that most districts and schools do not plan as they do not know "what needs to be done, where to begin, or how to do it" (p. 2).

School-based strategic planning begins with an assessment process to determine what currently exists (needs assessment) and what needs to exist (areas of improvement) in terms of educational legislation, always focusing on better student achievement. A strategic planning process provides a process: how to begin, what data to collect and from whom, analysis of the data and capacity building for educators through professional improvement, development of strategies to reach goals and objectives, as well as evaluation measures to ensure the plans are working.

STRATEGIC PLANNING PROCESSES

While strategic planning is necessary for improving educational outcomes, in the past the focus was strictly on assessment-based outcomes; however, school systems and schools need to consider complex and evolving demands from parents, students, educators, and community stakeholders; economic competition from charter and virtual schools; environmental (changes in demographics), political (demands for increased student achievement), societal (expectations to address social justice issues), and technological (infrastructure needs and hardware and software costs) demands; the need to build teacher capacity; instructional planning processes; and requirements of continually changing legislation at the state and national levels.

The strategic planning process is cyclical and iterative, deliberate and functional. Strategic planning is systematic as it requires stakeholders to state who, what, why, where, when, and how and then to provide the criteria for addressing each of the elements. Strategic planning is also a rational plan because it forces stakeholders to consider cause and effect; to consider the ends before considering the means; order the steps while seeking continuous feedback. Strategic planning is systematic because there are phases through which to logically progress, though not necessarily in a linear fashion. While there are opportunities for planners to proceed in a direct line, some decisions may necessitate the use of pauses, during which a review of desired outcomes may be necessary. Chan (2010) suggested strategic planners needed to have the "right direction … to the right extent … to the right moment" (p. 5), noting that, ultimately, the success was dependent on the human element needed to implement the plan.

Table 1.1 Strategic Plan Components and Processes

1.	Identification of needs using a need assessment
2.	Analysis of needs assessment data
3.	Development and prioritization of achievable goals and objectives
4.	Developing strategies (what, when, how) to reach goals and objectives
5.	Addressing and building capacity (professional development)
6.	Implementing strategies to reach targeted goals and objectives
7.	Monitoring, evaluation, and assessment of implementation of the strategic plan
8.	Ongoing evaluation to determine success

CONCLUSION

Initiative and compliance fatigue have plagued schools since the passage of No Child Left Behind in 2001. With punitive measures attached to improving performance, schools and school systems were forced to assess student achievement in terms of quantitative performance numbers and quickly adopt measures to improve performance within the measure of the school year. School leaders and teachers charged with achieving targeted goals within a 9-month school calendar usually focused on solutions premised on professional development and tied to the purchase of federally funded instructional materials. There was little focus on root causes, no time to gather input from community members, and little time for teachers to address underperforming students. The process of planning strategically to improve student achievement provides promise.

Strategic planning is a process, and though all stakeholders may have input, just having a strategic plan does not mean the plan is successful. Strategic planning is a process of self-analysis; the process ensures the focus is on students. However, ultimately measurements and accountability for all stakeholders (leaders, teachers, students, parents, and stakeholders) is critical. The planning process necessitates data gathering, establishing goals and objectives, establishing strategies to reach the goals, and establishing a timeline.

IMPLICATIONS FOR SCHOOL LEADERS

Strategic planning is not a quick fix. It takes time to initiate the strategic planning process, build commitment to become involved in the process, engage stakeholders, build capacity, implement strategies, assess outcomes, and evaluate the results to determine if what was planned is working; continuous improvement is a process. With time constraints short for schools who are working with strategic planning processes, strategic planning requires commitment.

Use of strategic planning processes allows schools and stakeholders to establish what is working successfully as well as not so successfully in order to address the needs of students. Once a needs assessment is completed and goals and strategies to reach the goals are established, the school leader is one key to success. The school leader needs to work side by side with stakeholders to ensure processes are established to execute the necessary assessments; professional development builds capacity in teachers; strategies are implemented with fidelity; and monitoring and evaluation processes take place. Without school leader support, there is very little chance the process of initiating a strategic plan and implementing it will be successful.

ESSA guidance promotes the need for strategic planning, a systemic planning process established to allow schools to do a needs assessment and develop their own mission (purpose) and vision (direction), analyze data from the needs assessment, develop strategies (actions to reach improvement goals), develop processes (to implement strategies), and ultimately monitor (accountability) and evaluate (accountability and performance indicators) stakeholder group involvement.

FOLLOW-UP ON VIGNETTE

As Anne Smith enters the high school to begin the new school year, she is relieved that her role as leader of a strategic planning process is over, or at least hopes it is. The strategic planning principals' committee worked for more than 2 weeks assembling information and recommendations for the superintendent.

The superintendent compiled all the information and submitted the draft strategic plan to the school board along with the committee's recommendations. The school board members were not happy. The superintendent had done little to prepare the board to receive his strategic plan, and they perceived they were left out of discussions.

Two board members approached Anne and asked for clarification about her role in preparing the recommendations. Now the board is bringing in an outside consultant to develop a strategic plan. Anne is confused. She performed the task asked of her and now finds herself with another dilemma. She thought she had done a good job in chairing the strategic planning process working with district principals. In light of the school board's response and school board members' questions about the recommendations the committee made to the superintendent, Anne is rethinking the strategic planning processes she used. What should have been done differently?

REFLECTION

Anne was given a limited time frame to initiate and work with a committee of principals on strategic planning; therefore, her focus was to complete the assigned task for the superintendent. In retrospect, Anne realized she could have taken the initiative to research strategic planning to make sure she was using best strategic planning practices. Conducting some research about strategic planning would have led to more understanding about the inclusion and involvement of different perspectives such as board members who might have been included in the strategic planning process. Initiating a conversation with the superintendent to make him aware of the strategic planning processes and potential issues that might arise if stakeholders other than principals were not involved would have been appropriate.

CHAPTER 1 QUESTIONS

1. Discuss the administrator's role in educating stakeholders on the need for a strategic planning process to be both systemic and cyclical (SLO1, SLO3, SLO5).

2. With strategic planning now a requirement with ESSA, contrast the benefits of ESSA's accountability requirements as compared to the previous requirements of NCLB (SLO2, SLO3, SLO4).

3. Describe how the process of developing a strategic plan is essential for guiding continuous school improvement and identify specific planning skills/leadership traits needed to orchestrate the strategic plan (SLO1, SLO2, SLO3, SLO4, SLO6).

REFLECTION AND APPLICATION

1. Think about how initial meetings with stakeholders need to present information about a school. How might a school leader best present and discuss data and the need for instructional improvement without assigning blame?
2. Create a short presentation for a community agency such as a Chamber of Commerce to discuss the importance of strategic planning and why there is a need to have community stakeholders involved.

REFERENCES

Beach, R. H., & Lindahl, R. A. (2007). The role of planning in the school improvement process. *Educational Planning, 16*(2), 19–43.

Beach, R. H., & Lindahl, R. A. (2015). A discussion of strategic planning as understood through the theory of planning and its relevance to education. *Educational Planning, 22*(2), 5–16.

Chan, T. C. (2010). The implications of symbols in educational planning: 2009–2010 presidential address. *Educational Planning, 19*(2), 1–7.

Eacott, S. (2008). Strategy in educational leadership: In search of unity. *Journal of Educational Administration, 46*(3), 353–375. https://doi.org/10.1108/09578230810869284

Elementary and Secondary Education Act of 1965 (ESEA), P.L. 89-10.

Every Child Succeeds Act (ESSA) of 2015, P.L. 114-95, S.1177, 114th Cong. (2015).

Fayol, H. (1916/1949). *General and industrial administration.* Pitman.

Harnack, J., & Seebaum, M. (2017). *Finding simplicity on the other side of complexity: A strategic planning process streamlines district work and improves the system for all.* McREL International.

No Child Left Behind Act of 2001, P.L. 107-110, 20 U.S.C. § 6319 (2002).

North Carolina Department of Public Instruction. (2016). *North Carolina school improvement guide.* https://files.nc.gov/dpi/documents/program-monitoring/planning/sip-guide.pdf

Rohm, H. (2008). *Balanced scorecard.* Balanced Scorecard Institute.

ADDITIONAL RESOURCES

Allison, M., & Kaye, J. (2015). *Strategic planning for nonprofit organizations: A practical guide and workbook* (2nd ed.). Wiley.

American Institute for Research and the National Association of Elementary School Principals. (2017). *Principals' action plan for the Every Student Succeeds Act: Providing all students with a well-rounded and complete education.*

Batel, S., Sargrad, S., & Jimenez, L. (2016). *Innovation in accountability: Designing systems to support school quality and student success.* Center for American Progress.

Bryson, J. (2011). *Strategic planning for public and nonprofit organizations* (4th ed.). Jossey-Bass.

Bryson, J. M. (2011). *Strategic planning for public and nonprofit organizations: A guide to strengthening and sustaining organizational achievement* (Vol. 1). Wiley.

Bryson, J. M., & Alston, F. K. (2011). *Creating your strategic plan: A workbook for public and nonprofit organizations.* Jossey-Bass.

Chenoweth, K. (2016). ESSA offers changes that can continue learning gains. *Phi Delta Kappan, 97*(8), 38–42. https://doi.org/10.1177/003172171664701

Council of Chief State Schools Officers. (2020). *State strategic vision guide.* https://ccsso.org/resource-library/state-strategic-vision-guide

Hanover Research. (2014). *Best practices for school improvement planning.*

Kaufman, R. A., & Herman, J. J. (1991). *Strategic planning in education: Rethinking, restructure, revitalizing.* Technomic.

McGuinn, P. (2016). From No Child Left Behind to the Every Student Succeeds Act: Federalism and the education legacy of the Obama Administration. *Publius, 46*(3), 392–415. https://doi.org/10.1093/publius/pjw014

O'Day, J. A., & Smith, M. S. (2016). *Systemic problems, systemic solutions: Equality and quality in U.S. education.* American Institutes for Research. http://www.air.org/sites/default/files/downloads/report/Equality-Quality-Education-EPC-September-2016.pdf

Patrick, S., Worthen, M., Frost, D., & Gentz, S. (2016). *Meeting the Every Student Succeeds Act's promise: State policy to support personalized learning.* International Association for K–12 Online Learning (iNACOL). https://aurora-institute.org/resource/meeting-the-every-student-succeeds-acts-promise-state-policy-to-support-personalized-learning/

Reeves, D. (2007). Making strategic planning work. *Educational Leadership, 65*(4), 86–87.

Rice, J. (2017). The disconnect between heralded business concepts and effective school leadership. *Educational Planning, 24*(2), 55–61.

Schanzenbach, D. W., Bauer, L., & Mumford, M. (2016). *Lessons for broadening school accountability under the Every Student Succeeds Act.* Brookings Institute.

Steiner, G. A. (2010). *Strategic planning.* Simon & Schuster.

Weiss, J., & McGuinn, P. (2016). States as change agents under ESSA. *Phi Delta Kappan, 97*(8), 28–33. https://doi.org/10.1177/0031721716647015

The Needs Assessment

VIGNETTE

Anne Smith had learned a lot since her initial foray into strategic planning. Now she was responsible for implementing strategic planning process at her school. She wanted to ensure stakeholders in her community were participants in the strategic planning process at her school. Anne had been trying to engage more stakeholders with the school, and attempts to engage parents and community stakeholders had not been very successful.

The first step was to conduct a needs assessment to gather input from teachers, staff, students, parents, and community members. She did not just want to send out surveys to school sites and get feedback from parents who always attended school events. She wanted to gather data from differing perspectives. Anne's school had changed a great deal in the past 10 years, and in the year since she had been the principal at the school, student demographics had changed.

Her school currently had more students who were English language learners (ELL) and more students were now qualifying for free and reduced lunches. Parents of ELL students did not often participate in school activities, but they sometimes came to school events when their children were receiving an award, if the event was held after hours. She also had a few community businesses listed as school partners who did not often participate in school events.

The Title I director said she needed to review the mission and vision listed in the school improvement plan as it seemed outdated, and she needed internal and external stakeholder participation in the revision. Anne realized before she started working with her faculty that she needed to do more research. Where could she obtain a needs assessment and learn how to conduct a needs assessment, and where did mission and vision fit?

LEARNING OUTCOMES

After reading this chapter, the learner should be able to do the following:

1. Describe the needs assessment process as part of the strategic planning process
2. Demonstrate knowledge and understanding about the differences in the roles of mission and vision
3. Discuss the need to incorporate internal and external stakeholders in the strategic planning process
4. Explain the differences in the perspective of internal and external stakeholders and why inclusions of differing perspectives are important to the strategic planning process

KEY WORDS

Needs assessment

Internal stakeholders

External stakeholders

Constituent groups

Community stakeholders

School community members

INTRODUCTION

Strategic planning is a problem-solving process. Effective strategic planning is not a quick fix. It takes time to initiate a needs assessment process, find and engage stakeholders, and build capacity in stakeholders to provide necessary input. Stakeholders are individuals or groups with interests in schools. A **needs assessment** provides a process to determine concerns from **internal** and **external stakeholders**. Internal stakeholders are those individuals and groups (such as faculty, bus drivers, and cafeteria workers) who work within the organization. External stakeholders are those who are affected by the performance of the organization and who do not work within the organization.

Paine and McCann (2009) reported **constituent groups** for schools are comprised of students, parents, school faculty, district staff members, school board members, businesses, community support organizations and churches, institutions of higher education, and public agencies. Internal stakeholders were defined as those working in the school or school system while external stakeholders were defined as those not working in the day-to-day role at a school, sometimes considered school-community partners, or **community stakeholders**.

STAKEHOLDER RELEVANCE

Involved stakeholders are invested stakeholders. A needs assessment provides a process to include and involve both internal and external stakeholders to systematically obtain information. McCawley (2009) stated that using needs assessment provides approaches, awareness, and outcomes; internal and external stakeholder knowledge provides information while explaining concerns and desired outcomes. Internal stakeholders have access to information and key data needed for needs assessment. External stakeholders provide different perspectives and are key to providing information about community expectations for schools. Internal and external stakeholders are all **school community members.**

Nonregulatory guidance on the Every Student Succeeds Act of 2015 (ESSA) specifically addresses the following question: "Which stakeholders can help identify local needs and/or root causes?" recommending the following:

> Local education agencies (LEAs) should engage in timely and meaningful consultation with a broad range of stakeholders (e.g., families, students, educators, community partners) and examine relevant data to understand the most pressing needs of students, schools, and/or educators and the potential root causes of those needs. Interviews, focus groups, and surveys as well as additional information on students (e.g., assessment results, graduation rates), schools (e.g., resources, climate), and educators (e.g., effectiveness, retention rates) provide insights into local needs. (p. 3)

Guidance from ESSA (2015) also notes,

> A needs assessment process … includes establishing a schoolwide planning team, clarifying the vision of school reform to identify school strengths and weaknesses, creating the school profile, identifying data sources for the needs assessment, and analyzing the collected data. (p. 13)

Needs assessment information includes obtaining data about schools from different resources. State education agency information provides demographic information: attendance, enrollment, graduation rates, dropout rates, special education data, student mobility, discipline referrals, safety data, and at-risk population information as well as state-based standardized assessment data. Both state-level data and district-level data may also include information about teacher certification, teachers with advanced degrees, and teachers with out-of-area certification.

District- and school-level data provides information on student learning and achievement specific to the school: grade levels, subjects, assessment trend information, staff attendance, and turnover rate. School and grade-level data can reference school subject area data, chapter and unit tests, quizzes, and student project information. School-level information can also include information on discipline referrals and school-climate data.

MISSION (PURPOSE) AND VISION (DIRECTION)

School leaders and school faculty and staff need to identify and clearly define their shared beliefs about teaching and learning as part of the local school district's mission. One of the initial steps in the strategic planning process is the need to clarify the mission of the organization, the school. The mission statement is a purpose statement specifying why the organization exists and, in educational terms, what the organization aims to accomplish. The vision statement is a short statement describing the organization's objectives. The vision sets the direction for the organization and specifies the objective the organization wants to reach.

The mission and vision are important components for the school organization and provide direction to achieve the established goals. Vision, also known as the direction, refers to the needed change, motivation, and coordination for action within an organization. Ultimately, a detailed vision guides the strategic plan and keeps all stakeholders on the same course.

Consensus for Purpose and Direction

Until all stakeholders have a full understanding and commitment to work toward a consensus for a shared mission and vision for the institution, progress and improvements will be limited. Communicating the need to align the day-to-day teaching and learning processes to long-term student achievement outcomes allows stakeholders such as parents and guardians to see where their roles fit and how they can contribute to meeting student achievement. Identifying core values and community influences that affect the school district is important as they often impact the mission and purpose. School leaders must understand the potential for mismatches in definition or perception from stakeholders while working to collaborate to formulate a statement of new direction.

Conducting a needs assessment provides a process for school administrators to gain information from both internal and external stakeholders. It is an exercise in communication, taking in information and analyzing it to gain perspective. Gaining stakeholder support is not an easy process. Everyone has an opinion and wants consideration for their viewpoints.

Parents often do not see the long-term view for student achievement and many times do not understand how day-to-day learning activities and long-range learning objectives are related to achieving student achievement. Providing communication to parents and gaining their support for student learning is a key process needed to ensure academic improvement progress is continuous.

CONCLUSION

Community stakeholders, taxpayers, want to see their return on the investment in education; stakeholders want their children to be successful 21st-century citizens. With decreasing revenues and increased expectations for student achievement, there are questions about methods schools can use to provide greater academic achievement success. Bringing community partners and stakeholders together provides methods to assess community resources available to support schools. Bringing stakeholders together provokes conversation and an exchange of perspectives, which may lead to dialogue about decision-making processes.

There will be different levels of stakeholder involvement: listeners who only listen; stakeholders who will listen at length and deliberate before engaging; and those with high levels of engagement and interaction. Multiple opportunities for stakeholder involvement are necessary. Some stakeholders will come to get specific answers; some will wait to see if stakeholder involvement is truly valued and if questions and concerns are welcomed. How can parents support their students? What resources are available in the community to support schools? What concerns do community stakeholders have for student outcomes in their district? What can community partners and organizations do to support better student achievement? Conducting a needs assessment provides information to align both community and school goals.

IMPLICATIONS FOR SCHOOL LEADERS

Often, school leaders are day-to-day school managers. Becoming involved in a strategic planning process forces school leaders to commit to become more involved community members. Identifying the needs of the school and finding methods to address those needs is an all-consuming process for a school administrator; a needs assessment provides an assessment process and provides data to support the need for personnel, programs, and services for students. A needs assessment also addresses internal needs to build capacity from the school perspective as well as a community perspective. Working in partnership with internal and external stakeholders provides a method for each element to see where they fit and to contribute to establishing collaboratively established goals and objectives.

FOLLOW-UP ON VIGNETTE

Anne Smith relied on her ability to gather data and develop consensus for her foray into strategic planning. She worked with the Title I director and called on faculty members from within the school and also faculty from the nearby university to augment her knowledge of the needs assessment process. She formed a committee from faculty who responded to her initial request to be members of the Strategic Planning Committee.

Anne also reached out to her community partners and has asked her faculty and staff members to submit the name of a community or church-based organization that she could contact to solicit more members. She also asked her school board for names of community members to include on the Strategic Planning Committee. She also contacted several other agencies in the district. Additionally, Anne asked a faculty member from a nearby university to facilitate the initial stakeholder meeting so that she could be engaged as an internal stakeholder in the first meeting. She was not totally sure how the strategic process needs assessment worked, but she felt that her participation in the process would be beneficial. She thought she had made a good initial beginning. What other community agencies and partners did she need to include?

REFLECTION

Anne made a great deal of progress in understanding strategic planning and how to initiate a school's needs assessment. Asking for help from university faculty who had experience with strategic planning was a good decision. Anne suspected that stakeholders could and would provide plenty of input, but ultimately, the educators needed to collect the needs assessment data, analyze it, organize it for use in prioritizing goals and objectives, and, finally, understand the strategic planning process.

One of the next tasks was to consider the processes necessary to analyze the information collected in the needs assessment and then to figure out how to connect the data to establishing realistic and measurable goals and objectives. Thinking about the types of data that might be collected and brainstorming with committee members might be a good beginning. She wanted to include diverse types of data but recognized that some of the information might provide short-term goals and objectives, while other data might take longer amounts of time.

CHAPTER 2 QUESTIONS

1. Formulate a list of data tools to be used in a school during a needs assessment and determine if the assessment tool reflects an internal perspective, external perspective, or both (SLO1, SLO4).
2. Identify the influences (internal and external) that impact the mission and vision of the school (SLO2, SLO3).
3. Stakeholder involvement is a major focus in ESSA. What are some ways to identify the needs and perspectives from a variety of stakeholders? Explain why the needs or perspectives of stakeholders should be addressed in the strategic planning process (SLO1, SLO3, SLO4).

REFLECTION AND APPLICATION

1. Reflect on school administrators with whom you are familiar. Given what you know about their responsibilities, explain how the school leader might best support the needs assessment process and provide two examples of the support process.
2. Interview two colleagues who work with the school improvement team. Ask them to identify examples of the current mission statement and vision statement "in action."

REFERENCES

Every Child Succeeds Act (ESSA) of 2015, P.L. 114-95, S.1177, 114th Cong. (2015).

McCawley, P. F. (2009). *Methods for conducting an educational needs assessment.* University of Idaho.

ADDITIONAL RESOURCES

Bottoms, G., & Schmidt-Davis, J. (2010). *The three essentials: Improving schools requires district vision, district and state support, and principal leadership.* Southern Regional Education Board.

Cashman, J., Linehan, P., Purcell, L., Rosser, M., Schultz, S., & Skalski, S. (2014). *Leading by convening: A blueprint for authentic engagement.* National Association of State Directors of Special Education.

Center on School Turnaround at WestEd. (2017). *Four domains for rapid school improvement: A systems framework.* http://www.centeronschoolturnaround.org/four-domains/

Council of Chief State School Officers. (2017). *Understanding federally required education policy needs assessments and maximizing their impact.*

Council of Chief State Schools Officers. (2019). *Let's get this conversation started: Strategies, tools, examples and resources to help states engage with stakeholders to develop and implement their ESSA plans.* https://ccsso.org/resource-library/lets-get-conversation-started

Curtis, R. E., & City, E. A. (2009). *Strategy in action: How school systems can support powerful learning and teaching.* Harvard Education Press.

DuFour, R., & Marzano, R. J. (2015). *Leaders of learning: How district, school, and classroom leaders improve student achievement.* Solution Tree Press.

Elementary and Secondary Education Act, P.L. 89-10, 79 Stat. 27 (1965).

Griffin, J. A., & Otter, K. (2014). *It takes a village: How stakeholder engagement is the key to strategic success* [Paper presentation]. PMI® Global Congress 2014, Phoenix, AZ.

Harnack, J., & Seebaum, M. (2017). *Finding simplicity on the other side of complexity: A strategic planning process streamlines district work and improves the system for all.* McREL International.

Layland, A., & Redding, S. (2017). *Casting a statewide strategic performance net: Interlaced data and responsive supports.* Building State Capacity and Productivity Center. http://www.bscpcenter.org/casting/

Louis, K. S., Leithwood, K., Wahlstrom, K. L., & Anderson, S. E. (2010). *Investigating the links to improved student learning: Final report of research findings.* Wallace Foundation.

U.S. Department of Education. (2016). *Non-regulatory guidance: Using evidence to strengthen education investments.* https://www2.ed.gov/policy/elsec/leg/essa/guidanceuseseinvestment.pdf

Witkin, B. R., & Altschuld, J. W. (1995). *Planning and conducting needs assessments: A practical guide.* SAGE.

NEEDS ASSESSMENT RESOURCE INFORMATION

Bryson, J. M., & Alston, F. K. (2011). *Creating your strategic plan: A workbook for public and nonprofit organizations.* Jossey-Bass.

Corbett, J., & Redding, S. (2017). *Using needs assessments for school and district improvement: A tactical guide.* Council of Chief State School Officers (CCSSO) and Center on School Turnaround. https://www.ccsso.org/sites/default/files/2017-12/Worksheets-from-Needs-Assessment.pdf

Gupta, K., Sleezer, C. M., & Russ-Eft, D. F. (2007). *A practical guide to needs assessment.* Pfeiffer. https://hientl.files.wordpress.com/2011/12/tnyc_a-practical-guide-to-needs-assessments.pdf

McCawley, P. F. (2009). *Methods for conducting an educational needs assessment.* University of Idaho.

CHAPTER 3

Analyzing Needs Assessment Data

VIGNETTE

Anne Smith walked out of the cafeteria of the school where she was principal. She was excited and confident about the strategic process needs assessment that had been conducted both in her school and with her community of stakeholders. There was certainly a lot of data to consider. Committee members (administrators, faculty, staff, parents, and community stakeholders) spent time determining what data was desired, how to best obtain the data, and from whom to attain the data. Additionally, the strategic planning committee had done a lot of organization before the needs assessment began, working with the local university faculty to figure out both the needs assessment processes as well as what to do with the data that was gathered and the processes needed for analysis.

Administrators, faculty, and staff collected school-based data (demographics, assessment data, and school-based data), while other committee members figured out how to best collect information from other types of stakeholders (parents, students [depending on age], businesses, school partners, as well as community groups and clubs). A great deal of the focus for the needs assessment was to determine the processes that should be used to gather the data (surveys, interviews, focus groups). Help from the nearby university had been essential for decisions needed about the data-gathering process. Additionally, university personnel volunteered to work with the data analysis process, both to ensure the analysis process went well as well as to provide perspective and objectivity.

LEARNING OUTCOMES

After reading this chapter, the learner should be able to do the following:

1. Define the differences in quantitative data and qualitative data
2. Define disaggregation of data
3. Discuss the use of graphic organization of data in a matrix
4. Explain categorical data that might be included in needs assessment
5. Discuss how the process of analysis might be accomplished with stakeholders

KEY WORDS

Disaggregation of data   Qualitative data
Quantitative data   Matrix
Gap analysis

INTRODUCTION

A well-designed and well-executed needs assessment lays the foundation for a strong strategic plan. Needs assessments provide a baseline of what exists in all organizations. Needs assessments should include both internal and external perspectives. ESSA requirements demand that

> a schoolwide program shall be based on a comprehensive needs assessment of the entire school that takes into account information on the academic achievement of children in relation to the challenging State academic standards, particularly the needs of those children who are failing, or are at-risk of failing, to meet the challenging State academic standards and any other factors as determined by the local educational agency. (ESSA Section 1114[b][6])

Processes to do needs assessments can include surveys, interviews, focus groups, and documents such as school and district improvement plans, annual reports, budgets, census data, and existing system and school improvement plans.

Legislative autonomy from ESSA to local school district leaders makes the results from the needs assessments critical to make data-based improvement plans and to set targets to capitalize on strengths and improve student achievement. After analysis of the assessment data, school leaders can begin directing their focus and prepare an evidence-based, measurable plan.

THE ANALYSIS PROCESS

Once all needs assessment data is collected, analysis of data is next. While there is no one correct process, it is important to consider what types of data have been collected in order to organize and disaggregate the data to make it easier to work with. In terms of school data, **disaggregation of data** refers to breaking down data into smaller categories and groups, sometimes called subgroups. There are different types of data and different sources of data.

Needs assessments produce both **quantitative** and **qualitative data**. It is necessary to have both types of data to gain a holistic view of a school or school system. Needs assessments provide information about what is working and identify needs (**gap analysis**). Quantitative data is usually classified in terms of numerical data. Quantitative data in terms of school strategic planning is typified by areas such as numbers or percentages in student demographics, test scores (classroom assessments, school assessments, or mandated state assessments), or frequency (promotion, retention, graduate rates).

Qualitative data is usually less structured data and cannot be displayed numerically unless predetermined ratings are assigned. Qualitative data is often descriptive information obtained in surveys, interviews, or focus groups. While not necessarily as objective in terms of numbers, qualitative data obtained from stakeholders provides perspective that may not be reflected in quantitative data.

USING STAKEHOLDERS IN THE ANALYSIS PROCESS

Using stakeholders as participants in the analysis process contributes to understanding the outcomes as well as the validity of the data. Dividing the analysis process into three tasks simplifies the process: (1) compilation and disaggregation; (2) sorting and organizing types of data; and (3) evaluating the data for making decisions.

Compiling the Data

One of the challenges in conducting a needs assessment is the different types of data that are obtained from conducting the needs assessment. Achievement, demographic information, program information, perceptions, as well as longitudinal data are a few of the data types that may be gathered.

A. Achievement data: Achievement data includes standardized test scores, report card data, and classroom-based assessment data.

B. Demographic data: Demographic data describes the student population in terms of enrollment, attendance, ethnicity, socioeconomic status, discipline and behavior, and information about students with limited English proficiency and about abled and disabled students.

C. Program data: Program data reflects information on types of academic programs: curricular and cocurricular.

D. Perception data: Perception data reflects information on the attitudes and beliefs of stakeholders, including teachers, students, parents, and community members. Perception data also includes information about academics, school leadership, quality of instruction, and school climate.

E. Longitudinal data: Longitudinal data provides information about change, both in short- and long-term data. Gathering and comparing longitudinal information provides information about trends and patterns in the data.

Sorting and Organizing Data

There is no one method to sort and organize data. Placing data into charts and tables are organizational methods facilitated by the use of a computer spreadsheet or **matrix** that allows the data to be displayed and sorted into different categories. Information is organized into rows and columns to display, possibly by rank order, or displayed longitudinally for comparison (Grochow, 2017).

Evaluating Data

Organizing the data into categories can be facilitated by setting up categories on a computer spreadsheet. Types of data can then be organized by categories that facilitate evaluation and understanding of the data: qualitative or quantitative data, student achievement data, demographic data, or socioeconomic information. Evaluating and understanding the data is easier when the data can be sorted and compared to assess differences.

Categorical data may include the following:

- Student demographic information (gender, race, ethnicity, disability, migrant status, English language learners, economically disadvantaged students, free-reduced lunch status, students in foster care, and homeless students)
- Assessment and achievement data: high-performing students (honors, advanced placement, gifted and talented) and low-performing students (subgroup performance, under-represented groups, diverse learners, special education)
- Attendance, truancy, disciplinary actions
- Culture and climate reports, safety reports
- Retention, promotion, graduation rates
- Support services (advising, counseling, transition services)
- Technology (hardware, software, infrastructure)

- Teacher quality, recruitment, and retention of teachers
- Planning and operation (physical structure needs)

Using a matrix or a spreadsheet allows organization of data into relationships. Grochow (2017) suggested categorical data might be organized by consideration of data types (demographic, academic performance, environmental, organizational, financial); interests (faculty, students, administration, community stakeholders); sources of data (primary [survey, interview, focus group] or secondary [assessment data]); types of data (qualitative or quantitative), and methods of presentation (table, graph, chart).

Assigning data to categories provides both a method to graphically display information and may provide ways to organize the information obtained from the data. Organization of the results allows consideration for what the data show and what the data means. Graphic displays also allow a method to establish a baseline that can be used to measure change.

CONCLUSION

The Community Tool Box developed by the Center for Community Health and Development (2017) at the University of Kansas summarizes the processes of developing strategic plans: assess, plan, act, evaluate, and sustain. The first process, conducting a needs assessment, is a crucial element in initiating and building a strategic plan. The needs assessment process provides data that gives insight into existing school and community factors; involving stakeholders in the needs assessment process provides credible evidence to show that the needs assessment process was inclusive. Guidance on the process for conducting a needs assessment from outside personnel allows faculty and staff members to take more objective roles both in doing the needs assessment as well as in analyzing data. Once the analysis of data is completed, developing and prioritizing goals and objectives is the next step.

IMPLICATIONS FOR SCHOOL LEADERS

School leaders need to take the responsibility to initiate needs assessment processes. Using personnel resources from outside organizations provides a method to ensure that the school leader's perspective does not color the assessment process as well as the analysis of data. Many school leaders feel they are capable of doing a needs assessment. However, stakeholders (teachers, staff, parents, community members, and school partners) provides inclusive perspectives that are necessary before attempting the work to design a strategic plan. Acceptance of the data as it exists is key, negative or positive.

FOLLOW-UP ON VIGNETTE

Anne Smith called on faculty from a university with which the district had ties to gather information on strategic planning processes. University members were excited about the liaison with a school and volunteered to work on the strategic planning process, guiding them through the different processes of gathering the needs assessment data. The needs assessment data reflected information from differing perspectives, and with the efforts of the neighboring university, analysis of assessment statistical data was not as difficult a process as it might have been.

The expertise of university faculty in organizing and putting the data collected in a spreadsheet matrix facilitated both the organization and analysis process. It had been critical for Anne, as the school principal, to play an objective role in the process of analyzing and then putting the data into a useable and realistic format that could be used to move forward for planning purposes. Not all the data was positive; some was downright unpleasant, as not all stakeholders (faculty, staff, parents, and stakeholders) felt the school was moving toward meeting the needs of students, and the data reflected that the needs of some students were not being addressed as well as they might be.

REFLECTION

Anne Smith's decision to use local university resources provided a starting point for the strategic planning needs assessment. She had solicited participation for using a needs assessment instrument provided by the university by attending opening of school meetings, asking for volunteer to work on the strategic planning and needs assessment processes, and also asking for their help in recruiting stakeholders from their school service areas. Anne wanted the data gathered in the needs assessment to be reviewed holistically as well as categorically. Thus, the analysis of the data was accomplished as a participatory process, lending credence to the data analysis. Some findings were readily evident; other findings were not so clear. The next procedure was to take the data and figure out what strategies needed to be implemented to target changes that were needed, to develop strategies to build capacity in targeted areas, and to figure out how to capitalize on the strengths indicated in the needs assessment.

CHAPTER 3 QUESTIONS

1. Justify the benefits for using qualitative data as well as quantitative data to thoroughly disaggregate and better understand the information gathered from a needs assessment (SLO1, SLO2, SLO4).
2. Data may not always reflect positive information. As an aspiring school leader, explain how you might prepare a presentation of existing data and address facts that may not reflect well on student achievement (SLO3, SLO4).
3. Data gathered in the needs assessment needs to be reviewed holistically as well as categorically. Explain and give two examples of why it is important to see the data from holistic and categorical points of view (SLO1, SLO2, SLO3, SLO5).

REFLECTION AND ACTIVITY

1. Reflect on this statement: "Many schools are data-rich and information-poor" (Slotnik & Orland, 2010, p. XX).
2. The district leader has stated, "Every decision we (leaders, faculty, staff) make in each school will be made from data." What professional development might you need as a new school leader on how to analyze and interpret data? Cite two examples.

REFERENCES

Center for Community Health and Development. (2017). *Community tool box: Tools to change our world*. University of Kansas. http://ctb.ku.edu/en/table-of-contents/assessment/assessing-community-needs-and-resources/conduct-concerns-surveys/main

Every Child Succeeds Act (ESSA) of 2015, P.L. 114-95, S.1177, 114th Cong. (2015).

Grochow, J. M. (2017). *Data-driven IT strategic planning for data-driven IT leaders: From novice to expert: Strategic planning data organization matrix* [Paper presentation]. EDUCAUSE Annual Conference 2017, Philadelphia, PA.

Slotnik, W. J., & Orland, M. (2010, May 6). Data rich but information poor. *Education Week*. http://www.edweek.org/ew/articles/2010/05/06/31slotnik.h29.html

ADDITIONAL RESOURCES

Allison, M., & Kaye, J. (Eds.). (2015). *Strategic planning for nonprofit organizations: A practical guide and workbook* (2nd ed.). Wiley. https://doi.org/10.1002/9781118769690

American Institute for Research and the National Association of Elementary School Principals. (2017). *Principals' action plan for the Every Student Succeeds Act: Providing all students with a well-rounded and complete education.*

Bottoms, G., & Schmidt-Davis, J. (2010). *The three essentials: Improving schools requires district vision, district and state support, and principal leadership.* Southern Regional Education Board.

Bryson, J. (2011). *Strategic planning for public and nonprofit organizations* (4th ed.). Jossey-Bass.

Bryson, J. M. (2011). *Strategic planning for public and nonprofit organizations: A guide to strengthening and sustaining organizational achievement* (Vol. 1). Wiley.

Cashman, J., Linehan, P., Purcell, L., Rosser, M., Schultz, S., & Skalski, S. (2014). *Leading by convening: A blueprint for authentic engagement.* National Association of State Directors of Special Education.

Center on School Turnaround at WestEd. (2017). *Four domains for rapid school improvement: A systems framework.* WestEd. http://www.centeronschoolturnaround.org/four-domains/

Chenoweth, K. (2016). ESSA offers changes that can continue learning gains. *Phi Delta Kappan, 97*(8), 38–42. https://doi.org/10.1177/0031721716647017

Council of Chief State School Officers. (2017). *Understanding federally required education policy needs assessments and maximizing their impact.*

Council of Chief State Schools Officers. (2020a). *Let's get this conversation started: Strategies, tools, examples and resources to help states engage with stakeholders to develop and implement their ESSA plans.* https://ccsso.org/resource-library/lets-get-conversation-started

Council of Chief State Schools Officers. (2020b). *State strategic vision guide.* https://ccsso.org/resource-library/state-strategic-vision-guide

Curtis, R. E., & City, E. A. (2009). *Strategy in action: How school systems can support powerful learning and teaching.* Harvard Education Press.

DuFour, R., & Marzano, R. J. (2015). *Leaders of learning: How district, school, and classroom leaders improve student achievement.* Solution Tree Press.

Elementary and Secondary Education Act of 1965, as amended by the Every Student Succeeds Act of 2015, P. L. 114-95 § 114 Stat. 1177 (2015–2016).

Griffin, J. A., & Otter, K. (2014). *It takes a village: How stakeholder engagement is the key to strategic success* [Paper presentation]. PMI® Global Congress 2014, Phoenix, AZ.

Hanover Research. (2014). *Best practices for school improvement planning.*

Harnack, J., & Seebaum, M. (2017). *Finding simplicity on the other side of complexity: A strategic planning process streamlines district work and improves the system for all.* McREL International.

Lane, B. (2009). *Exploring the pathway to rapid district improvement.* Center on Innovation and Improvement. http://www.adi.org/downloads/Exploring_the_Pathway_to_Rapid_District_Improvement.pdf

Layland, A., & Redding, S. (2017). *Casting a statewide strategic performance net: Interlaced data and responsive supports.* Building State Capacity and Productivity Center. http://www.bscpcenter.org/casting/

Louis, K. S., Leithwood, K., Wahlstrom, K. L., & Anderson, S. E. (2010). *Investigating the links to improved student learning: Final report of research findings.* Wallace Foundation.

O'Day, J. A., & Smith, M. S. (2016). *Systemic problems, systemic solutions: Equality and quality in U.S. education.* American Institutes for Research. http://www.air.org/sites/default/files/downloads/report/Equality-Quality-Education-EPC-September-2016.pdf

Patrick, S., Worthen, M., Frost, D., & Gentz, S. (2016). *Meeting the Every Student Succeeds Act's promise: State policy to support personalized learning.* International Association for K–12 Online Learning (iNACOL).

Reeves, D. (2007). Making strategic planning work. *Educational Leadership, 65*(4), 86–87.

Rice, J. (2017). The disconnect between heralded business concepts and effective school leadership. *Educational Planning, 24*(2), 55–61.

Schanzenbach, D. W., Bauer, L., & Mumford, M. (2016). *Lessons for broadening school accountability under the Every Student Succeeds Act.* Brookings Institute.

Steiner, G. A. (2010). *Strategic planning.* Simon & Schuster.

U.S. Department of Education. (2016). *Non-regulatory guidance: Using evidence to strengthen education investments.* https://www2.ed.gov/policy/elsec/leg/essa/guidanceuseseinvestment.pdf

Weiss, J., & McGuinn, P. (2016). States as change agents under ESSA. *Phi Delta Kappan, 97*(8), 28–33. https://doi.org/10.1177/0031721716647015

Witkin, B. R., & Altschuld, J. W. (1995). *Planning and conducting needs assessments: A practical guide.* SAGE.

NEEDS ASSESSMENT RESOURCE INFORMATION

Bryson, J. M., & Alston, F. K. (2011). *Creating your strategic plan: A workbook for public and nonprofit organizations.* Jossey-Bass.

Center for Community Health and Development. (2017). *Community tool box: Tools to change our world: Assessing community needs and resources.* University of Kansas. http://ctb.ku.edu/en/table-of-contents/assessment/assessing-community-needs-and-resources/conduct-concerns-surveys/main

Corbett, J., & Redding, S. (2017). *Using needs assessments for school and district improvement: A tactical guide.* Council of Chief State School Officers (CCSSO) and Center on School Turnaround. https://centeronschoolturnaround.org/wp-content/uploads/2018/04/NeedsAssessment-Final.pdf

Gupta, K., Sleezer, C. M., & Russ-Eft, D. F. (2007). *A practical guide to needs assessment.* Wiley. https://hientl.files.wordpress.com/2011/12/tnyc_a-practical-guide-to-needs-assessments.pdf

McCawley, P. F. (2009). *Methods for conducting an educational needs assessment.* University of Idaho.

CHAPTER 4

Developing and Prioritizing Goals and Objectives

VIGNETTE

Principal Anne Smith was deep in thought when her assistant principals Mary Johnson and Clarke Holmes walked into her office after school had dismissed for the day. This time of the day was usually reserved for the school administrators to touch base on the multiple events taking place at the high school, including strategic planning. While the principal was the titular leader, both assistant principals Mary and Clarke were taking the lead in participating in ongoing meetings that were addressing the results of the needs assessment; Clarke was serving in the strategic manager role.

Needs assessment results were not huge surprises; community stakeholders wanted graduates who were ready for the workforce, parents wanted students ready for postsecondary education or employment, teachers wanted to produce students who could function in the 21st-century world, and students wanted to make an impact in some facet of their world. All were worthy endeavors; each goal had its challenges. Their next job was to determine strategic goals, determine prioritization of strategic goals, and ultimately establish a course of action and strategies to address each.

As the principal, Anne was grateful that faculty and community and parents had been participants in the strategic planning process, although it had taken longer than she had initially planned to go through the strategic planning processes. Everyone had taken the process seriously, and each wanted to ensure differing points of view were included and wanted success for their students. The next steps were to lead stakeholders in the process of developing and prioritizing goals.

LEARNING OUTCOMES

After reading this chapter, the learner should be able to do the following:

1. Define the key words
2. Explain the necessity of establishing priorities for goals
3. Elaborate on the need to establish limited numbers of goals
4. Explain why collaborative processes are needed in establishing goals
5. Discuss the process of developing goals
6. List the components of SMART goals

KEY WORDS

Prioritizing   Sense making
Goal   SMART goals

INTRODUCTION

Once an analysis of the data obtained in the strategic planning needs assessment is completed, developing and **prioritizing** goals is the next process. A **goal** is defined as an aim or a purposeful objective toward achieving an end result. One of the goals in the strategic planning process was the involvement of stakeholders with the end goal that while coming from differing perspectives, stakeholders could collaboratively work together to gather knowledge about the school and gain a background of contextual knowledge about school improvement goals as well as school achievement. Goal setting provides a communicative tool for both stakeholders and faculty to collaboratively set goals to provide a vision for school success. However, the strategic planning needs assessment may provide too many goals to address in terms of school improvement. Too many goals may lead to lack of success in reaching any goals; thus, the number of goals needs to be limited and focused for increasing student achievement.

Newman (2012) describes goal setting processes as methods to increase faculty productivity. Those involved in the strategic planning process need to be participants in the consideration of possible goals to provide perspective on direction and focus. Collaborative participation from strategic planning members and faculty changes the communication process in a school. The process promotes shared conversations about success and understanding of what is needed to achieve goals (Leithwood & Jingping, 2018).

School improvement goals need to be aligned to address improvement areas noted in the strategic planning needs assessment. Researchers such as Elmore and Burney (1997) suggested the need for collaborative processes of decision making: "Shared expertise is the driver of instructional change" (p. 16). Frank and Hovey (2014) advocated a systems approach considering setting goals based on a return in investment in education and student achievement: "How can we use all our limited resources strategically to improve student achievement and meet our goals[?]" (p. 3). Anderson (2006) suggested school administrative leaders are key to setting goals by making evidence-based decisions about establishing goals that are in the best interests of schools.

COHERENCE AND SENSE MAKING IN SETTING GOALS

Coherence in goal setting, **sense making**, is essential to the process of establishing goals. Researchers Mandinach et al. (2008) and Lai and Schildkamp (2013) equated the establishment of goals as a process of sense making. Sense making, in reference to school performance, is the process of constructing knowledge, based on prior and current data from the strategic plan needs assessment data, in order to establish goals. According to Sleegers et al. (2009), sense making "is shaped by interactions with others who are directly and indirectly engaged in the same endeavors, and how school leaders' sense-making shapes strategic choices and influences their leadership practices" (p. 154).

Schildkamp (2019) notes that there are not always obvious solutions to setting goals; however, goal setting based on needs assessment data provides methods to establish "clearly defined, specific and measurable goals" (p. 258). While collaboratively establishing goals and objectives based on stakeholder input, educational expertise is warranted in making judgements about establishing the number of goals as well as establishing methods and strategies for reaching goals to improve student achievement.

GOAL CHARACTERISTICS

Marzano et al. (2001) suggested strategic planning goals need to have the following characteristics: developed with consensus, few and focused, clearly stated, data based, measurable, connected to stakeholders' desired outcomes, systemic, sustainable, and attainable. One of the overriding issues in goal setting is an initial reaction to push to quickly reach goals without considering a prioritization process and the need to ensure that the implementation expectations are understood (Sinay et al., 2016).

The strategic plan needs assessment analysis provides a method to consider prioritization of goals to achieve improved student achievement. There may be multiple areas to be targeted; however, prioritization of goals needs to be based on a guiding question: What is the one strategy that will have the most impact on student achievement? In most cases, the key element for improvement is based on improving a faculty's professional capacity to achieve all targeted areas for improvement.

Considerations for priority are also needed: Why is the goal important, and how will the goal be accomplished with manageable and actionable steps tied to timelines and to available resources? Timelines need to outline steps in the process to reach the goal, and timelines should be keyed to the school calendar with measurable steps. The temptation to establish too many goals, too fast, without thorough preparation, without addressing faculty capacity, though well intentioned, can be overwhelming for faculty and lead to failure.

Once the goals are prioritized, goal language needs to be addressed. **SMART goals**, visioned by George Doran (1981) were targeted to processes needed to provide a method from a management viewpoint to address goal setting. Doran suggested that it was necessary to connect the goal to an action plan. According to Doran, criteria for goals needed to be specific, measurable, achievable, research based, and time related—SMART goals. Doran also noted that every goal might not have each criteria but provided guidance for writing goals.

Strategic planning processes promote shared meanings between stakeholders and more complete understanding of the "issues under consideration and the action taken by the organization" (Jalonen et al., 2015, p. 2796). With stakeholders involved and providing input in the strategic planning process, stakeholders can understand strategic planning processes as a method to improve student achievement outcomes.

However, the development of clear and measurable goals, building capacity to implement strategies to reach the goals, implementing strategies, and providing resources needed to meet goals also need to involve faculty members and school leaders who are involved in reaching goals. School leaders have expertise related to both assessment of performance in relation to school improvement as well as observing and interpreting teaching and achievement processes taking place in their schools.

Methods to set up goal prioritization might include using a chart to establish the following elements: goal, action, responsibility, timeline, monitoring processes, method(s) of evaluation.

Goal Prioritization Chart

GOAL	PRIORITY	ACTION	RESPONSIBILITY	TIMELINE	MONITORING	EVALUATION
What is the goal?	How important is it?	Capacity to implement?	Who will implement?	When?	How often? Process? By whom?	When? Process? By whom?

Two processes factor into the prioritization process: (a) identification of goals and (b) decision making. Identification of the goals is based on the data provided through the needs assessment. Decision making requires educators to determine the complexities of the processes needed to reach the goals and rank them by priority. Prioritizing needs to be done by the educator stakeholders who have a grasp of the educational processes needed to reach the goals. Regardless of the processes used to develop the goals and prioritize the goals, without support needed to reach the goal, the goal-setting processes are incomplete. Faculty must have the capacity to provide and use strategies needed to reach the goals. Additionally, commitment is an issue, both from leadership and faculty. Unless there is faculty commitment about why the goals are important and an understanding of the value of reaching the goals, there will be little chance of success.

CONCLUSION

School improvement processes have been an emphasis since No Child Left Behind (2002) was initiated with goals to improve student performance. Despite enormous emphasis on improving student achievement and the punitive processes attached to lack of improvement, there was little success in improving student achievement in all performance areas. One of the tenets of NCLB was that it was a top-down legislative movement with little collaboration on goal setting or processes to reach goals and not enough time to develop capacity and resources to support teachers, who were charged with meeting goals within a school calendar year.

The strategic planning process is a method to approach improvement from building support from stakeholders. The process is intended to be inclusive with those involved to build improvement based on the perspectives of many. However, educators are still charged with implementing envisioned goals. If there is an absence of support to build the capacity of educational faculty, the process will not be successful.

IMPLICATIONS FOR SCHOOL LEADERS

Ultimately, the leader is the responsible party for guiding the processes to move from the provision of data from the needs assessment to translating the data into consideration for goal setting. Effective school leaders are critically connected to the ultimate success of goal development and goal setting. Without an emphasis from the leader to inclusive representation of faculty to build consensus on goal directions, there is little chance of success. If there is a discrepancy in what the faculty believes currently exists and what needs to exist, there is little chance that school leaders can develop goal-relevant behaviors in faculty.

FOLLOW-UP ON VIGNETTE

Mary Johnson and Clarke Holmes walked into Anne Smith's office after school had dismissed for the day at Middlestone High School. As day-to-day strategic planning manager, Clarke led the processes to establish the strategic planning goals and to prioritize goals. It had taken 6 months to get all the goals established, but the goals were finally finished, and a sense of purpose and conversation about goal priorities were a part of the daily conversations among teachers. Inclusion of faculty and strategic planning committee members in developing and prioritizing goals had been a key component. Now that goals were settled, the leadership team needed to meet again to consider the next step in the process: consideration of the resources available to initiate the strategies to reach the goals. This afternoon, Anne, Mary, and Clarke needed to review calendars so that all participants could stay informed and set meeting dates.

REFLECTION

While it would be easier in many ways for the school leaders to take over the goal-setting processes, to do so would negate all the work and collaborative processes in which stakeholders had participated. It is ultimately the responsibility of the school leaders to ensure that the strategies are initiated. At this point, the leadership team reflected on the fact that they had finally been able to get most of the faculty to work together and to consider different perspectives. The process had provided the school leadership team with an increased sense of efficacy about their leadership roles and the processes necessary to guide school improvement.

The frustrating part of the strategic planning process was that the process moved more slowly than they wanted, and there were pitfalls, and sometimes it was overwhelming in terms of how everything would come together. However, what was also evident to the three school leaders was the process of working together had made them more knowledgeable about the challenges of school improvement and had also made them stronger in their knowledge about what it would take in the future to succeed in reaching the goals that had been set. As leaders, they acknowledged to one another that the strategic planning processes were also building their skills to support the faculty in the school improvement processes.

CHAPTER 4 QUESTIONS

1. Sense making, prioritizing, and limiting goals in the strategic planning process allows for focus, achievability, and sustainability. Define the school leader's role in finalizing the understanding, priority, and number of goals for continuous improvement within the school (SLO1, SLO2, SLO3, SLO4).
2. As a school leader, what factors (internal and external) need to be considered when developing a goal? What strategies can be used to ensure collaboration with stakeholders to determine the goals (SLO1, SLO4, SLO5)?
3. Using the goals in a current school plan, evaluate each one and identify the SMART components. If the goal is missing any of the SMART components, further develop the goal to address what is missing (SLO1, SLO5, SLO6).

REFLECTION AND APPLICATION

1. Consider the following issue: Determining which goals need to be addressed may depend on the needs of the faculty in terms of teacher capacity. As a school leader, how might you systematically improve the capacity of teachers to address their own needs?
2. As the school leader, it is your job to lead the work with goal setting. List five competencies a leader should possess in order to lead the goal-setting process and propose a plan with two examples to improve your own competencies as a future school leader.

REFERENCES

Anderson, S. E. (2006). The school district's role in educational change. *International Journal of Educational Reform, 15*(1), 13–37.

Doran, G. T. (1981). There's a SMART way to write management's goals and objectives. *Management Review, 70*(11), 35–36.

Elmore, R., & Burney, D. (1997). *Investing in teacher learning: Staff development and instructional improvement in community school district #2.* Consortium for Policy Research in Education and National Commission on Teaching & America's Future, Teachers College, Columbia University.

Frank, S., & Hovey, D. (2014). *Return on investment in education: A "system-strategy" approach*. Education Resource Strategies. https://www.erstrategies.org/library/return_on_investment_in_education

Jalonen, K., Schildt, H., & Vaara, E. (2018). Strategic concepts as micro-level tools in strategic sensemaking. *Strategic Management Journal, 39*(10), 2794–2823.

Leithwood, K., & Jingping, S. (2018). Academic culture: A promising mediator of school leaders' influence on student learning. *Journal of Educational Administration, 56*(3), 350–363.

Lia, M. K., & Schildkamp, K. (2013). Data-based decision making: An overview. In K. Schildkamp, M. K. Lai, & L. Earl (Eds.), *Data-based decision making: Challenges and opportunities* (pp. 49–67). Springer.

Mandinach, E., Honey, M., Light, D., & Brunner, C. (2008). A conceptual framework for data-driven decision-making. In E. Mandinach & M. Honey (Eds.), *Data-driven school improvement: Linking data and learning.* (pp. 13–31). Teachers College Press.

Marzano, R., Pickering, D., & Pollock, J. (2001). *Classroom instruction that works*. Association for Supervision and Curriculum Development.

Newman, R. (2012). Goal setting to achieve results. *Leadership, 41*(3), 12–16, 38.

Schildkamp, S. (2019). Data-based decision-making for school improvement: Research insights and gaps. *Educational Research, 61*(3), 257–273. https://doi.org/10.1080/0013188 1.2019.1625716

Schmoker, M. J. (2004). Tipping point: From feckless reform to substantive instructional improvement. *Phi Delta Kappan, 85*(6), 424–432.

Sinay, E., Ryan, T. G., & Walter, S. (2016). *Research series on school effectiveness and school improvement: Goal setting* (Research Report No. 16/17-05). Toronto District School Board. https://www.tdsb.on.ca/Portals/research/docs/reports/CharacofEffectiveSIP.pdf

Sleegers, P., Wassink, H., van Veen, K., & Imants, J. (2009). School leaders' problem framing: A sense-making approach to problem-solving processes of beginning school leaders. *Leadership and Policy in Schools, 8*(2), 152–172. https://doi.org/10.1080/15700760902737162

CHAPTER 5

Choosing Strategies to Reach Goals and Objectives

VIGNETTE

Principal Anne Smith was considering how she and her administrative team might lead their faculty to develop strategies to address improvement in student achievement. For the most part the faculty had been participants in the strategic planning process; however, some of the faculty were extremely resistant to addressing the issues uncovered in the needs assessment. Anne had encouraged some of the more reluctant faculty members to consider the needs of the students from a different perspective. While they were not enthusiastic about change, her faculty were student supporters, and all of them stated that they wanted to be responsive to addressing student needs.

Now it was a matter of figuring out how to choose some of the strategies necessary. Anne was struggling about the choice of strategies to address their students. She had done some research. Much of the information about strategy formation primarily came from the field of business; education was different. She had met with the superintendent and the federal programs supervisor who reminded her that the Every Student Succeeds Act required use of strategies tested with students. ESSA language called strategies "evidence-based practices," and she and her staff needed to review recommended strategies and practices the federal programs supervisor had pointed out to them.

The Strategic Planning Committee had completed the initial work: conducting a needs assessment, analyzing the data provided from the needs assessment, and prioritizing goals and objectives. The next step was to consider review and make final choices about recommended strategies. She was worried because she felt community stakeholders on the strategic planning committee were concerned about implementation of strategies that met their children's needs, rather than just adopting a list of strategies proposed by a federal agency. There were so many decisions to be made, and while faculty and community stakeholders could provide information and feedback, ultimately the decision-making processes about the strategies came back to her. She wanted to talk to her academic leadership team, and then she needed some time to think and make final decisions.

LEARNING OUTCOMES

After reading this chapter, the learner should be able to do the following:

1. Define the key words
2. Explain the process of considering and adopting strategies
3. Demonstrate knowledge about decision-making processes

KEY WORDS

Goals   Strategy/strategies
Objectives   Decision making

INTRODUCTION

With the goal of strategic planning in schools to continuously improve student achievement, strategic planning becomes the catalyst for reaching student achievement outcomes. The strategic planning process allows organizations to become proactive rather than reactive in that there is a common sense of direction and expected outcomes for the organization.

Isobel Stevenson (2019) reported,

It has often been noted that while all organizations have a mission statement, not all of them have a mission. Just so, while most organizations have a plan, few of them have a strategy. A plan is just an account of who will do what and when. By contrast, a **strategy** is a tight, cogent set of ideas about how best to fulfill the mission of the organization. It provides context, goals, and priorities, giving people a sense of *how* they should implement the plan and what it will take to do so successfully. (p. 62; emphasis added)

Goals in strategic planning are statements of expected outcomes; strategies are the approaches and methods use to reach the academic **objectives**. Adoption of strategies focused on deficiencies found in a needs assessment analysis provides increased opportunities for improvement as strategies are chosen to reach short- and long-term objectives for achievement.

Strategies (both organizational and instructional) are defined as deliberate and intentional measurable actions chosen to achieve objectives. Strategy choice involves the necessity to choose and/or develop methods to create competence to achieve the objectives, to ensure the resources and strategies are aligned, and to evaluate if the strategies have been implemented and are meeting the targeted goals. Strategies need to be established in terms of measurable objectives: understandable, obtainable, with planned steps not only to implement strategies but also to build capacity in teachers to implement the strategies and follow up to ensure teachers are implementing strategies appropriately and correctly.

Seminal literature about strategies (Mintzberg, 1987) stated developing strategies are not easy, suggesting that both planning and patterns need consideration. In terms of planning, a plan of action needs to be established with clearly designed strategies. Mintzberg also pointed out that organizations often have patterns of **decision-making** processes, often readopting past strategies used before as the processes are familiar, even though they may not be aligned to what is currently needed.

It is necessary to communicate to all faculty and staff the processes to be used, the implementation procedures, expectation for participation in terms of professional learning and implementation, and follow-up and evaluative processes. Strategies need to be aligned to achievement goals. Additionally, expectations are for all faculty, staff, and school leaders to be participants in the professional learning and implementation process.

School leaders need to role model, both in the professional learning and in the implementation processes (Lemoine et al., 2014):

> When principals are enthused and excited about their schools, generally, they are helping the students, faculty, and staff become more involved in translating the vision into goals. Principals may improve faculty awareness of their desire to lead instructionally through their enthusiasm. This instructional leadership includes the principal's role in staff development programs, facilitating and training teachers, and supporting new instructional techniques in the classroom. The principal's participation in professional development sends a message to the faculty that the information is important, and they will be expected to implement the strategies that are being presented. Principals serving as

instructional leaders must have a clear vision for their school and must be focused on the students and their specific needs. Typical goals for accomplishing a student-focused vision might include identifying strategies to meet the learning needs of all students, helping teachers adjust to a constantly changing school population, and increasing students' academic achievement. (p. 20)

When school leaders are not participants, there is less commitment from faculty. When school leaders demonstrate their commitment by involvement, there is more respect for the adoption process. A key part at this point is that school leaders need to ensure that procedures for implementation are completed prior to initiation of professional learning and refined during professional learning as faculty become familiar with strategies.

School leaders also need to make the commitment to provide follow-up, support, and modeling for faculty and staff. Commitment includes providing follow-up professional learning, support to build capacity for faculty and staff, resources for modeling and support, and, finally, frequent evaluative processes to ensure progress is being made to reach academic achievement goals.

DECISION MAKING

A major caution for school leaders is to consider every initiative that is currently in place. Stevenson (2019) reports reviewing current initiatives is important; "trying to do too many things at once" (p. 62) will not allow successful implementation of new strategies. One of the issues for school leaders is the need to review and decide which initiatives may need to be removed before adding new ones.

Decision-making processes require consideration of school level and district, state, and federal programs that may be affected by operational decisions to change initiatives, as well as consideration of the internal (school) and external (community) environment (Benjamin, 2014). Developing strategies include defining the scope of the strategy and matching the choice to the environment in which it will be used and to the capacity of those implementing the strategies. The planners and the school leaders have to ultimately make decisions about what to do and how to do it (Heller, 2019).

Strategy choices involve seven steps: (1) identifying the issue; (2) gathering data to make well-informed decisions; (3) analyzing the data; (4) considering strategy choices; (5) determining which strategies are needed; (6) developing an implementation process; and (7) evaluating implementation (Learning Point Associates, 2004). Once strategy choice decisions have been made for the implementation of strategies, it is important to address commitment.

Commitment for implementation of strategies affects operational decisions. School leaders and faculty control the process of choosing strategies, consideration of the design of the strategies, the resources to implement the strategies, and the processes needed to implement. Choosing strategies requires further essential decision-making responsibilities: delineation of the processes necessary for faculty to implement. The nature and the magnitude of implementing strategies is connected to expectations for intended behaviors of faculty as part of their job descriptions.

Planning for implementation of strategies includes choosing and defining the strategies; ensuring faculty agree to the use of the strategies (commitment); ensuring that strategies are observable, measurable, and doable; aligning the steps to be taken to ensure strategies are implemented; and specifying what evaluative criteria will be used to ensure the strategies are successful. Without consistency and stability of the school leader's support for implementation, reaching targeted academic achievement objectives will be inhibited. Additionally, commitment for implementation of strategies is also a commitment to the need to build teacher capacity; professional development is integral to short- and long-term success.

STRATEGY CHOICES

Choice of strategies chosen depends on targeted achievement objectives. Learning Point Associates (2004) provided guiding questions for defining specific strategies:

- Clear and understandable to all readers and users?
- Dependent on other activities? (If so, be sure to describe the sequence of actions.)
- Based on best practices?
- Observable and measurable?
- An action that will make a positive difference?
- One specific action or activity?
- An activity that will definitely lead to accomplishing the goal?
- One that all team members endorse?
- Assignable to specific persons?
- Doable (one that can be implemented)? (p. 19)

CONCLUSION

The analysis of the strategic planning needs assessment provides community and faculty stakeholders information about the academic areas that need improvement. Once the information is available, it is up to the Strategic Planning Committee and faculty to consider myriad choices for strategies to address academic deficiencies. The choices made by the strategic planners form a total school strategy: what the school wants to achieve in the future and their plan to get there.

While the committee can make recommendations for goals and objectives, ultimately, school leaders have to make operational decisions. Since NCLB there have been mandates for schools to add initiatives for improvement. NCLB required quick turnarounds that promoted success. Rarely did schools have time to make a realistic needs assessment, consider what steps needed to be accomplished, plan for professional learning, implement selected strategies, and take the time to support faculty and staff to make successful use of recommended strategies.

Under NCLB, schools were required to make plans, implement plans, and be evaluated within a 9-month school year based on their choices. Evaluations came quickly and judgements were often harsh. Too often initiatives were started and with short timelines for implementation, never put into action before additional initiatives were added. With the strategic planning process, all the current initiatives that are in place need to be considered. School leaders need to make decisions about priorities, consider all the factors involved, and make decisions about what implementation processes are critical to the operational success of the implementation processes.

IMPLICATIONS FOR SCHOOL LEADERS

School leaders have a multifaceted role. While managing the plan and all the resources, the intent for the school leader is to be an instructional leader. With strategic planning, there are expectations for community members and faculty and staff to provide input for the needs assessment and then consider the results of the needs assessment. The role of the school leader in the strategic planning process is to consider the evidence provided in the needs assessment and then to consider what needs to be accomplished.

If the strategic planning committee and faculty provide context to what needs to happen to ensure better student achievement outcomes, the role of the school leader is to support the process. Ultimately, this support is another decision-making process. School leaders also have to model commitment to the process. For the plan of action to be a success, school leaders should be participants during professional learning; participatory leadership includes involvement and commitment to be a part of the process.

FOLLOW-UP ON VIGNETTE

Anne felt good about the strategies chosen to address the needs that were found in the needs assessment analysis. The process had taken faculty and community stakeholders through a review of evidence-based practices suggested for adoption. What worked for the faculty was that they went back to looking at their needs assessment and their SWOT analysis (strengths, weaknesses, opportunities, and threats) to match the chosen strategies to their desired outcomes, both short term and long term, and chose strategies to reach the outcomes.

There were many areas that needed improvement, but the guiding piece for each strategy selected had been what specific strategy could be used to make a real and measurable difference for students. Faculty members used a backward design process to consider and narrow down how many strategies they might implement at one time. The overriding factor was to implement any strategy for improvement; it was necessary to improve teacher capacity.

Faculty also reported concerns about too many initiatives along with past improvement implementations already mandated that might hinder achieving their goals and objectives. Anne knew that some initiatives were not working, and as the school leader she needed to review and remove initiatives that did not belong in the newly adopted strategies. With the strategic planning process, committee members, and faculty working together, she felt they had been able to choose the most effective strategies to reach the desired academic outcomes for their students.

REFLECTION

The literature on school leadership reports that the principal is the most influential factor in creating school success; they are responsible for designing and constructing an environment conducive to learning. School leaders (principals) were traditionally administrative managers rather than instructional leaders in the school. Principals are still building and resource managers, in charge of public and community relations, fundraisers, busing, meals, and discipline, while tending to school finances. However, with the passage of No Child Left Behind (2002), the principal moved from a management role to an instructional leadership role; school leadership expectations changed.

Principals are expected to establish a vision; to recruit and hire teachers; to motivate teachers and students through establishing high expectations; to demonstrate instructional leadership skills with academic content and pedagogical techniques; and to facilitate professional development while enabling the collection and analysis of data, ensuring teachers use data to drive student achievement, ultimately ensuring school operations run smoothly.

The school leader has a critical role in working with teachers, students, and parents to provide a better education for students. Current educational reforms demand the principal's participation in their implementation. Lemoine et al. (2014) list the following as school leader essential behaviors:

1. The effective leader sets the direction and establishes a vision to reach academic goals.
2. Effective principals have high expectations for teacher and student performance, articulating performance standards for teaching and learning.
3. As an instructional leader, the principal works with curriculum and instruction; the school leader presents focused and ongoing professional development, encourages instructional innovations, utilizes proactive change processes, and frequently monitors and evaluates teachers and student learning.
4. The effective school leader communicates and builds relationships with teachers who become part of the leadership team. Leadership is distributed among team members who are working collaboratively toward the same goal.
5. School leaders establish a safe, orderly, and positive environment and school culture in which learning can occur.
6. School leaders manage time wisely, promote the school in the community, attend school events, have a presence throughout the school interacting with students, faculty, staff, parents, and community members, and, thus, work long hours.

While still expecting consideration for economic, demographic, and technological factors that influence student academic outcomes, school leaders are expected to be accountable for school and student performance as well as meeting mandates for reform.

CHAPTER 5 QUESTIONS

1. Using the seven steps to determine a strategy, prepare a presentation to a group of stakeholders asking for support of the strategies. Explain why the strategies need to be considered as a part of a strategic plan (SLO1, SLO2, SLO3).

2. According to Mintzberg (1987), organizations often revert to patterns in decision-making processes based on familiarity instead of usefulness. Identify a current school strategy that needs to be revised and propose a new strategy more aligned with newly determined goal and objectives (SLO1, SLO2, SLO3).

REFLECTION AND APPLICATION

1. Consider what experiences you have had in learning new strategies to increase student achievement. Cite one positive example and an example of one experience that was not as positive. Explain the differences from your perspective and how a school leader can work toward better outcomes.
2. How might the school leader examine responsibilities of existing school improvement committees and determine adjustments based on current needs assessment data (student feedback, teacher feedback, parent feedback, culture audit, etc.)?

REFERENCES

Benjamin, S. (2014). Shifting from data to evidence for decision making. *Phi Delta Kappan*, *95*(7), 45–49. https://kappanonline.org/shifting-from-data-evidence-decision-making-school-improvement-benjamin/

Heller, R. (2019, September 23). Making sense of education policy at the state level: A conversation with Sara Dahill-Brown. *Phi Delta Kappan*, *101*(2), 36–41.

Learning Point Associates. (2004). *Guide to using data in school improvement efforts: A compilation of knowledge from data retreats and data use at Learning Point Associates*. https://schoolturnaroundsupport.org/sites/default/files/resources/guidebook.pdf

Lemoine, P. A., Greer, D., McCormack, T. J., & Richardson, M. D. (2014). From managerial to instructional leadership: Barriers principals must overcome. *New Waves-Educational Research and Development*, *17*(1), 17–30.

Mintzberg, H. (1987). The strategy concept: Five Ps for Strategy. *California Management Review*, *30*(1), 11–24. https://doi.org/10.2307/41165263

No Child Left Behind Act of 2001, P.L. 107-110, 20 U.S.C. § 6319 (2002).

Stevenson, I. (2019). An improvement plan is not enough—you need a strategy. *Phi Delta Kappan*, *100*(6), 60–64. https://kappanonline.org/school-improvement-plan-not-enough-you-need-strategy-stevenson/

Building Capacity

VIGNETTE

Anne Smith was reviewing plans for implementing strategies needed to increase student academic performance. Building capacity in teachers to accomplish their goals and objectives was not so easy as simply scheduling professional learning sessions. The strategic plan process demanded that she lead the process to build capacity by modeling her commitment to the process. She knew that if she was not an enthusiastic participant and supporter in the professional learning process, there would be little commitment from the faculty.

Anne's consistent support of the strategic planning process was key. The choice of professional development activities was to build capacity for everyone to carry out the plans, to make connections between goals and outcomes, timelines, responsibilities, as well as accountability processes. Using the analysis results from the needs assessment plan had provided faculty and staff impetus to use the ESSA best practices to target improvement areas and suggest the strategies chosen.

Now her priorities were to ensure that the professional learning sessions were focused on providing faculty with the knowledge and skills they needed to address targeted competencies. It was not simply a matter of providing information about strategies and assigning strategies to teachers; there was a real need to provide examples and model actual application for faculty, support them, and monitor progress.

Finding the time and the money to build faculty capacity was an additional task. Teachers needed to be provided dedicated time to collaborate and align lessons along with support during the initial use of strategies. Providing time and resources for collaboration to work on planning for implementation and support to use newly acquired strategies showed commitment from the school leader to building success. As the school leader she also needed to build trust in teachers to support the development and facilitation of their skills.

If teachers felt they were working in isolation and without support, there might be little use of the strategies. She and the leadership team needed to review the master schedule to rework and add collaborative work sessions with resources to cover classes in order to provide support for planning and implementation, to ensure in-school coaches were involved in the implementation and support, and also to identify problems and barriers.

LEARNING OUTCOMES

After reading this chapter, the learner should be able to do the following:

1. Define the key words
2. Discuss the capacity-building processes
3. Demonstrate knowledge about the process of building capacity

KEY WORDS

Capacity building   Continuous improvement
Professional learning   Professional learning communities
Professional capital

INTRODUCTION

The need to continue to build pedagogical abilities in teachers and the ability to improve their practice continues to be a critical need for improving student achievement (Darling-Hammond et al., 2017). **Capacity building** is the process to improve or increase the ability of faculty to implement strategies to continuously improve student learning and achievement. Termed as professional development, **professional learning** and capacity building are also referenced as collective or personal learning or building **professional capital**. Building capacity includes the processes of formal and informal learning, collaborative and individual practice, feedback, and follow-up activities intended to develop, extend, and supplement "an individual's skills, knowledge, expertise and other characteristics as a teacher" (Organization for Economic Co-operation and Development [OECD], 2009, p. 49).

Darling-Hammond et al. (2017) stated effective professional development "is content focused; incorporates active learning; supports collaboration; uses models of effective practice; provides coaching and expert support; offers feedback and reflection; is of sustained duration" (p. 7). **Continuous improvement** in terms of building capacity is the process of focusing on improving educational quality through systemic efforts to improve student learning (Bryk et al., 2015).

Educators need different strategies, tools, and processes to improve student learning; thus, the focus for continuous improvement is to build instructional abilities in the educators who are working with students. The process of building educator capacity is cyclical; processes are chosen to build educator capacity: (1) Coherent goals and objectives for achievement are defined; (2) professional development is targeted to building capacity tied to meeting learner needs; (3) collaborative responsibilities and tasks are elaborated for faculty and school leaders; (4) support for implementation of targeted strategies is provided through professional learning, collaborative planning, and coaching in the implementation of strategies; (5) strategies are implemented in context with professional standards and daily instructional practices; (6) follow-up coaching and support is provided; and (7) frequent review of data provides accountability for the implementation process both in terms of building capacity as well as in outcomes for student achievement. Ultimately, the capacity-building process is built on the targeted goals established from the strategic planning needs assessment.

There is a substantive need for collective accountability in the process of building what Fullan et al. (2015) termed professional capital. The cycle of learning requires the necessity to establish coherence in terms of the vision and definition of goals, while building collective capacity, and then frequently reviewing data to provide accountability for the process of building capacity.

An additional process is the acceptance of the responsibility for student learning by all faculty as well as leaders. Building leaders need to demonstrate their commitment to implementing collaborative processes through consistent participation in professional learning, protecting time for collaboration and coaching, applying strategies to improve student learning, and modeling their involvement, thus building trust in the process.

Collective accountability requires expectations for accountability in terms of continuous improvement; all school members are responsible for meeting learner needs. Expectations include investments in personal learning for all, use of professional standards of practice to establish curriculum based on learner needs, and requirements for collaboration both in terms of lesson planning, delivery, and assessment. Acceptance of responsibility also includes the need to address what happens when students are not performing satisfactorily. DuFour (2004) addressed responsibilities for student achievement in terms of four questions:

1. What do students need to know?
2. How will we know they learned it?
3. What do we do when students have not learned what they need to know?
4. What about students who have already reached mastery?

DuFour (2004) established a formal process using **professional learning communities** (PLCs). A professional learning community process builds capacity as it provides a systemic process for supportive collaboration to build collective capacity. DuFour et al. (2008) defined the process as "educators committed to working collaboratively in ongoing processes of collective inquiry and action research to achieve better results for the students they serve" (p. 14).

DuFour also suggested the need to incorporate a reflective process, time for teachers to consider and share in their work processes. Incorporating reflection about strategy implementation along with working collaboratively to integrate new content strategies provides a more successful process according to DuFour (2004). DuFour and Reeves (2016) promoted the need for working in teams; working together on curriculum, developing assessments, and using data from assessments provides teachers methods to provide support for students who need more intervention to succeed.

PROFESSIONAL LEARNING PROCESSES

The process of building capacity in terms of costs are significant in terms of providing time for professional learning, professional learning resources, supporting follow-up, and establishing evaluative processes to determine success (Nguyen & Hunter, 2018). There are barriers to schools trying to adopt evidence-based processes suggested by ESSA; costs to build capacity are a consideration for school leaders. However, teachers may not feel confident about skills and use of skills; without investment in on-site support and follow-up, teachers may not implement planned strategies and an implementation gap can be created (Ferguson, 2019).

Effective professional development builds capacity in teachers in ways designed to enhance their instructional effectiveness. Implementation is two-phased. The first phase involves knowledge acquisition by the principal and faculty concerning the fundamentals of using the strategies as effective instruction. Professional learning provides shared learning experiences that enable faculty to speak a similar language and share common experiences. The second phase involves incorporating the acquired practices into daily instructional practices throughout the school.

Professional learning does not guarantee expertise in implementation of strategies and assessment of strategy outcomes. Professional learning can guide innovation and assist faculties in undertaking the changes necessary for improvement by encouraging the application of instructional innovations and the development of individual teaching techniques.

Teachers may not be as reluctant to try new strategies when school leaders encourage the use of new strategies that model the desired changes. The implementation then becomes viable through improving staff members' instructional practices in their interaction with students. Thus, faculty and staff members working in a supportive environment may not feel as constrained in the implementation of strategies.

Even though faculty may have instructional content regarding strategy implementation, follow-up, support, and monitoring need to take place to ensure implementation of strategies; if follow-up, support, and monitoring do not take place, the failure to use and implement strategies will constrain the ability to make academic improvements.

School leaders face challenges that force action when pathways to improve student achievement are unclear. There is strength, flexibility, and sustainability of improvement if the leader commits to the inclusion of all school members in building professional capital, including collaboration in professional learning, assigning responsibilities, and communication.

Building capacity in faculty to handle the complexities of adding new strategies and implementing them is also important. Critical skills for implementation in faculty requires follow-up and support processes, and implementation processes will require planning for use, creativity, and practice with all who are involved.

CONCLUSION

School leaders need a systemic process designed to build professional capacity for continuous school improvement. Scheduling professional learning sessions will not promote the need to build capacity for change and improvement in student learning. Establishing coherent and cohesive processes for building professional capacity is necessary, which involves multiple opportunities for learning, planning, and application. Support for the application of strategies with follow-up, support, and collaboration needs to be established and supported along with expectations for a continuous cycle of learning.

The adoption of recommended evidence-based practices provides methods to find best-practice strategies. However, teachers may lack confidence in recently acquired strategies and need follow-up and support from peers. Shared learning, professional learning, and collaboration promote teacher capital and provide a structure to support teachers as they implement newly learned strategies to improve student achievement. Teachers working together to support one another in professional learning provides an environment for collaboration and a climate of professionalism.

IMPLICATIONS FOR SCHOOL LEADERS

Building professional capital requires establishing a strategic planning process that is coherent. Building capacity also necessitates a commitment to develop skills for everyone involved in the learning process, and finally, building faculty capital facilitates a change in thinking and behaviors. Once capacity improves, there is empowerment for educators (Sacks, 2017).

Rather than taking direction, faculty members realize that they can set directions for themselves, the students, and the school as professionals (Stringer, 2013). This also means that school leaders relinquish their authoritative role and build collective responsibility, a process of shared leadership. Shared leadership responsibilities transform the culture of the school as school leaders and faculty capacity increases (Buttram & Farley-Ripple, 2016).

FOLLOW-UP ON VIGNETTE

Building capacity in teachers is a change process. Anne felt that faculty were more engaged and responsive in their own learning as a part of the strategic planning process. She and the leadership team had worked to ensure that the professional learning processes had been aligned to meet the desired outcomes for student learning. Anne regarded it as a systemic process; one professional learning session was not satisfactory. Long-term improvement was only reached through continuous professional learning, which leads to increasing the collective efficacy of all faculty members.

One of the best processes they had used was to involve the strategic planning committee and faculty and staff in the planning for professional learning. Faculty determined how best to time professional learning sessions. Anne involved the faculty both for accountability purposes as well as to facilitate trust in the process to reach the outcomes needed. While not formally acknowledging the process as shared leadership, Anne allowed faculty and in-school instructional coaches to establish a professional learning calendar, while she kept control over the cost of the resources and the structures needed to facilitate the timing of the professional learning sessions.

Anne learned more about her leadership team and faculty during the process of strategically planning professional learning. She also asked them to consider and reflect on potential barriers they might face in the implementation process. It was the decision of the faculty to share the potential barriers, to collaborate with their peers, and to problem solve so they could list alternatives if there were problems.

Anne realized not every problem had been covered; however, she and her leadership team had remained participants and listeners in the problem-solving sessions. Faculty appeared to be more creatively involved and willing to collaborate when they were essential to establishing a professional development process that impacted their own professional capacities.

REFLECTION

Shared leadership is not an easy process for school leaders; however, establishing shared leadership decision making is an outcome of the strategic planning process. Fostering a culture of professionalism and empowerment in their own learning allows teachers to grow productively and to feel empowered.

To be effective as a school leader, it is necessary to realize that the support and participation of faculty and staff in the process of working toward continuous school improvement is critical for success. School leaders often face vital decision-making processes. Including faculty and staff in the decisions in which they play a critical role positions everyone to be more responsible for accountability in terms of student learning.

CHAPTER 6 QUESTIONS

1. Explain how professional development, professional learning, and professional capital build capacity and are essential to the strategic planning process (SLO1, SLO2).
2. Evaluate a goal from a school improvement plan using the seven cyclical steps for continuous improvement by rating scale. Provide recommendations for the steps that need improvement and how these adjustments will help build capacity when applied to the strategic planning process (SLO1, SLO2, SLO3).
3. How might a professional learning committee (PLC) assist the school leader in building capacity and developing a commitment to continuous improvement? What barriers can impact the collaboration between the PLC and the school leader (SLO1, SLO2, SLO3)?

REFLECTION AND APPLICATION

1. Reflect on the following statement: "When members of a team make the results of their common assessments transparent, analyze those results collectively, and discuss which instructional strategies seem most effective based on the actual evidence of student learning, they're using the most powerful catalysts for improving instruction" (DuFour & Mattos, 2013, p. 38). Is this process currently used in your school? As a school leader, how might you make this happen?

2. Leadership matters. "To date we have not found a single case of a school improving its student achievement record in the absence of talented leadership" (Louis et al., 2010, p. 9). Provide two examples of talented leaders under whom you have worked or read about and cite evidence of their ability to improve student achievement.

REFERENCES

Bryk, A. S., Gomez, L. M., Grunow, A., & LeMahieu, P. (2015). *Learning to improve: How America's schools can get better at getting better.* Harvard Education Press.

Buttram, J. L., & Farley-Ripple, E. N. (2016). The role of principals in professional learning communities. *Leadership & Policy in Schools, 15*(2), 192–220. https://doi.org/10.1080/1570 0763.2015.1039136

Darling-Hammond, L., Hyler, M. E., & Gardner, M. (2017). *Effective teacher professional development.* Learning Policy Institute.

DuFour, R., & Mattos, M. (2013). How do principals really improve schools? *Educational Leadership, 70*(7), 34–40. http://www.ascd.org/publications/educational-leadership/ apr13/vol70/num07/How-Do-Principals-Really-Improve-Schools%C2%A2.aspx

DuFour, R. (2004). What is a "professional learning community"? *Educational Leadership, 61*(8), 6–11.

DuFour, R., DuFour, R., & Eaker, R. (2008). *Revisiting professional communities at work: New insights for improving schools.* Solution Tree Press.

DuFour, R., & Reeves, D. (2016). The futility of PLC lite. *Phi Delta Kappan, 97*(6), 69–71. https://doi.org/10.1177/0031721716636878

Education First. (2015). *Giving teachers the support and feedback they deserve: Five essential practices.*

Ferguson, M. V. (2019, September 23). The opportunities and challenges of ESSA's evidence-based requirements. *Phi Delta Kappan, 101*(2), 60–61.

Fullan, M., Rincon-Gallardo, S., & Hargreaves, A. (2015). Professional capital as accountability. *Education Policy Analysis Archives, 23*(15). http://dx.doi.org/10.14507/epaa.v23.1998

Louis, K. S., Leithwood, K., Wahlstrom, K., & Anderson, S. E. (2010). *Investigating the links to improved student learning: Final report of research findings.* https://www.wallacefoundation. org/knowledge-center/Documents/Investigating-the-Links-to-Improved-Student-Learning.pdf

Nguyen, T. D., & Hunter, S. (2018). Towards an understanding of dynamics among teachers, teacher leaders, and administrators in a teacher-led school reform. *Journal of Educational Change, 19,* 539–565. https://doi.org/10.1007/s10833-017-9316-x

Organization for Economic Co-operation and Development. (2009). *Creating effective teaching and learning environments: First results from TALIS.*

Sacks, A. (2017). Empowering teachers to respond to change: With high levels of change expected, schools must set up structures that help teachers share their best thinking and manage change effectively. *Educational Leadership, 74*(9), 40–45.

Stringer, P. (2013). *Capacity building for school improvement: Revisited.* Sense Publishers.

CHAPTER 7

Implementation

VIGNETTE

At last the school had moved into the implementation phase of the strategic plan. As the school leader, Anne was extremely proud of the faculty. The process had been comprehensive: needs assessment, analysis, planning, professional development, and collaboratively planning targeted strategies for school improvement as the initial implementation phase of their continuous school improvement process.

Findings from the needs assessment reflected the necessity to improve student engagement through strategies such as the integration of technology. Faculty members chose the strategies, participated in the professional development processes intended to facilitate the use of technology, and collaboratively planned the implementation process. Everyone knew there were not going to be any quick fixes, and they were all aware that implementers would face challenges; however, teachers were eager to implement the selected strategies.

Stakeholders in the strategic planning process agreed it was important not only for teachers to try out the strategies but also for the strategies to be used in a phased implementation with established checkpoints. Teachers also wanted quick checks on progress so they could make adjustments. While there were initially daily and weekly checks for the initial operationalization process, formal implementation reviews were established for 30, 60, and again at 90 days. Implementers felt that at the first 30-day review they would not have much data; at subsequent reviews, they would gain more data and have a more detailed picture of how the implementation and strategies were working.

LEARNING OUTCOMES

After reading this chapter, the learner should be able to do the following:

1. Define the key words
2. Discuss implementation processes
3. Discuss challenges faced when implementing new initiatives
4. Discuss fidelity of implementation

KEY WORDS

Initiatives

Strategies

Execution

Implementation

Fidelity of implementation

Strategic manager

INTRODUCTION

School leaders need to have expertise about planned school improvement processes and the operationalization of school improvement **initiatives** as well as be involved in decisions about what to execute, which strategies to implement, and implementation. These processes are challenging for schools, and leaders who excel connect the vision for what the school wants to achieve and the execution of the strategies to succeed and communicate them to everyone in the organization.

Strategies, execution, and implementation are not the same things; each has a different definition and involves different activities, tools, and people. **Strategies** are the specific processes to be used with students; **execution** reflects the decisions concerning what strategies are going to be implemented versus those not to be implemented, and **implementation** is the process of carrying out the use of the strategies (Schmoker, 2006; Sull et al., 2015).

Execution strategies need to be driven by the implementers, and teachers need to understand their roles and responsibilities in the implementation process (Loeb & Plank, 2008). One of the main processes in planning to execute is to narrow which strategies are key to achieving the student achievement desired. Ensuring faculty have the capability to execute the strategies (professional development) and providing the support and resources (follow-up) to ensure the faculty can execute what is necessary is also critical for implementation success.

IMPLEMENTATION OF STRATEGIES

Marzano (2011) suggests implementation of strategies can be accessed at four levels: beginning, developing, applying, and innovative. The beginning level reflects the initial process for a teacher who is just beginning to learn how to use a strategy. At the beginning level, teachers are unsure and may need support in the inclusion of the strategy and how to use it in the lesson. The development level shows movement past the beginning level to the process of planning and using a strategy in a lesson. The application level indicates that strategy use is at a point where the teacher is less dependent on how the strategy is to be used and more focused on interaction with students while using the strategy. The innovative level reveals that the teacher has moved to the ability to adapt and modify the strategy for lesson use. Developing fluency with use of strategies is essential as gains are not made with student achievement until the implementer has enough fluency to adapt the strategy, adjusting to meet students' needs. Follow-up on professional development and support, in terms of resources, is needed as teachers phase in new strategies.

With stakeholder participation in the strategic planning process, top-down directives should not drive the implementation process. The strategic planning process is based on needs assessment findings, which determine goals and objectives. Execution and implementation strategies should be chosen to meet goals and objectives by faculty who are directly implementing the processes.

Clarifying what is going to be done as well as what is not going to be done is necessary: Materials to be used, teacher behaviors to be demonstrated, and student activities need clarification (LaTurner & Lewis, 2013). Implementation is also based on faculty behaviors: Faculties need to understand what they are doing, how to do it, why they are doing it, as well as how to assess that the implementation process is working as it was planned. Additionally, managing implementation milestones is necessary before scaling up implementation. The implementation process also includes assessing implementation fidelity.

FIDELITY OF IMPLEMENTATION

The process of strategically planning the implementation of targeted improvement strategies should be a managed process. **Fidelity of implementation** is a concern: Are strategies being used? Are strategies used frequently? If teachers do not know how to use the strategies, is there a support system in place to model and demonstrate how strategies should be used, and how often?

Hanover Research (2014) reports that implementation data should include examination of implementation fidelity. Using a checklist that monitors explicit use of adopted strategies is warranted. Checking on strategies to be implemented, if strategies have been implemented, as well as how they are being implemented, and assessing the adherence to the intent of the planned strategies ultimately leads to implementation success. Data from a checklist provides information for which teachers need follow-up and support to reinforce how to implement strategies. Professional development follow-up with modeling and step-by-step practice promotes teachers' fluency levels in using strategies.

INITIATIVE FOCUS

Educators often work with multiple initiatives with no consideration of the complexity, size, and cumulative effects of them. It is necessary to prioritize and align initiatives to prevent overload for implementers. There can be multiplier effects when faculty working in multidisciplinary fields are involved in an additional or new implementation process. Oversight needs to be established to ensure there is alignment of initiatives and faculty are not involved in trying to implement multiple initiatives due to working in multidisciplinary subject areas. One method is to establish a school administrator or instructional coach as a **strategic manager** in charge of day-to-day implementation processes.

The strategic manager provides oversight on a daily basis as well as oversees long-range adoption processes. The strategic manager is also responsible for ensuring that there are no additional work expectations or unexpected conflicts during an implementation process. Addressing student achievement priorities requires a need for alignment. With teachers often working in multidisciplinary fields, it is important to establish priorities, especially when a new initiative is beginning. Milestones need to be established in terms of daily, weekly, and monthly timeframes. Thus, implementation can focus on the chosen strategies, assessment of data, meeting milestones, and determination of expansion.

The key for implementation is that each person who is implementing a strategy has to actually do the implementation. Ensuring that the implementation process takes place is a challenge for faculty. There should not be so many expectations for faculty to accomplish that implementation does not actually take place. The process for implementation also includes the need for back-up plans to cover emergencies. Without a back-up plan, loss of an implementer places more burdens on others, and execution and initial implementation processes may not happen. If the execution does not take place, re-establishing priorities and work expectations need to be addressed.

Capacity is the issue with back-up planning. Building capacity for implementation necessitates planning how to cover classes if implementing teachers are not present. Including substitutes in the training process can provide back-up. "New improvement strategies do not always guarantee increases in student achieve-ment, but partial implementation and inconsistent implementation will most certainly doom even the best strategies [and programs] to failure" (Dean & Pars-ley, 2010, p. 1).

The most critical responsibility of the strategic manager is problem solving. To ensure alignment and knowledge of day-to-day decisions, the strategic man-ager needs to establish quick operational meetings each week, review strategies in planned sessions each month, and have execution meetings as needed. One of the benefits of having someone in the formal alignment role is clarity between the imple-mentation process and implementation milestones. Additionally, decision making at the implementation level and decision alignment at the school administrator or instructional coach level keeps bottom-up processes as priorities.

CONCLUSION

The strategic planning process is designed to focus on outcomes. As profession-al development takes place, challenges to implementing and executing strategies need to be discussed. As the level of the school expands from elementary school to middle and junior high school to high school, there are increasing challenges for implementation. Additionally, key processes include defining who is respon-sible for execution; educators not involved in the implementation process should not be decision makers.

Consideration of how current initiatives and the addition of other initiatives will interface with current teacher responsibilities is critical; existing initiatives and teacher responsibilities with initiatives need review. The needs assessment findings should include what exists in terms of initiatives in terms of teacher responsibilities. Consideration of faculty responsibilities needs to include the following:

- If a new or additional initiative will be a factor in conjunction with what already exists
- If initiatives can be modified or dropped
- If existing initiatives cannot be modified, how newly adopted initiatives can be factored into the ability of faculty to implement in the existing timeframe for classes

Initiating a new process at a school is challenging. Establishing a new initiative as a piloted, phased-in process permits faculty to acquire mastery of the strategies they are implementing as well as allows follow-up professional development for the implementation process along with in-class modeling. Crafting the scaling-up process in stages is key to success and to sustaining the processes.

IMPLICATIONS FOR SCHOOL LEADERS

School leaders need to keep the essential outcomes in mind when an initiative implementation is planned. While the school leader may not manage the implementation on a day-by-day basis, communication between strategic managers and the school leaders is essential. The school leader has to be able to articulate what is underway and why and be knowledgeable about challenges faculty face during implementation. Multiple initiatives can derail the execution of the strategies.

Three issues are of immediate concern: First, there needs to be a comprehensive assessment of what exists. Data from existing initiatives need to be considered and data reflecting success in promoting achievement need to be compared. If current initiatives have not made an impact on student achievement, then data from existing initiatives needs review and reconsideration. Logical decision making is required based on the data. Some initiatives may need to be terminated. The school leader needs to recognize and make decisions or deal with lack of execution.

Second, in adding initiatives, faculty input needs to be considered. Without buy-in from faculty, there will be initiative inertia. Reeves (2006) reported that schools with the most success in student achievement had pared down initiatives to usually less than six. Demands from national, state, and district offices meant that there were often too many competing initiatives to be successful in any or all of them.

Finally, teachers need to have the ability to build levels of success in using strategies to reach goals and objectives. While quickly scaling up abilities of faculty is desired, initiatives need to be considered in terms of what faculties can accomplish within the given time frame and within a given number of school days. Deep implementation is considered an ideal state but probably will not take place immediately.

Implementation should be a planned process; making sure that teachers know what to do, how to do it, and that the process is having the outcomes that are targeted is key to success. The focus needs to stay on the processes determined to be key through monitoring the implementation process, providing support and resources, and using data to support the decision-making process.

FOLLOW-UP ON VIGNETTE

There were constant challenges with implementing the strategies designed to engage students through the use of technology. Faculty who were part of the phase 1 initiation were prepared to execute the strategies. The strategic manager was closely following the initiation processes and monitoring teachers to ensure they felt supported. Still, the initiation was a part of the many facets of school life.

The leadership team investigated all the school initiatives and were diligent in affirming that initiatives were focused and critical for student success. However, they did not catch every barrier for implementation, and there were still department-, grade-, and subject-level initiative requirements that had gone unrecognized. Catching each barrier to implementation was a work in progress.

Anne felt that faculty were more engaged and responsive in their own learning as a part of the strategic planning process. Because the implementation was phased in, Anne regarded it as a systemic process; based on the data available, teachers were becoming more fluent in using the strategies, and students recognized the efforts made on their behalf.

Communication with faculty, staff, and stakeholders had been critical in the implementation. There were deliberate processes established to keep Anne as the school leader, and students, faculty, and stakeholders were informed about what was taking place. While some faculty were challenged in the initial implementation phase, others were becoming more fluent in the use of the strategies.

Monitoring and evaluation were key to ensure success of the project. Additionally, there was a constant need to keep capacity levels as high as possible. There were many events and programs at the school, including substitutes in the training who had helped to supplement when faculty members had to be absent or became ill. Additionally, faculty became problem-solvers. They foresaw problems and worked with one another to address challenges.

REFLECTION

School leaders are often reminded of their responsibilities in improving student achievement. Since the passage of No Child Left Behind, schools have been responsible for making every effort that was recommended to improve student achievement. This meant that initiatives were usually top-down mandates added each year to meet targeted goals. Researchers have reported that despite the initiatives put into place through No Child Left Behind mandates, there were few long-term continuous school improvement successes.

Schools had good intentions; however, each year brought new mandates for improvement and new initiatives. Rarely were initiatives removed. Thus, layer after layer of reform meant teachers were challenged to use everything in past initiatives as well as to implement new ones. With the number of school days and the number of hours in a school day unchanged, teachers were challenged to meet disparate goals of differing initiatives. Making an assessment of initiatives in subjects, departments, and grade levels is critical if there is to be a change of focus and a chance to succeed in meeting goals and objectives.

Once a needs assessment is made, it is important to focus on the implementation of the most important current priorities; other initiatives may need to stop, requiring letting go. When this does not happen, researchers such as Fullan (2006) and Reeves (2006) referenced the problem as initiative fatigue. Fullan used the term "initiativitis" and suggested there was a tendency to launch an endless stream of disconnected initiatives that no one could possibly manage. Findings in the needs assessment should reflect what initiatives are taking place; when new goals and objectives are determined, older initiatives need to be discarded.

CHAPTER 7 QUESTIONS

1. When implementing a strategic plan, differentiate the importance of each element (strategies, execution, and initiatives). What is the school leader's responsibility for each to promote continuous improvement (SLO1, SLO2, SLO3)?

2. Explain why the school leader cannot and should not be the strategic manager for the implementation of the new initiatives or strategic plan (SLO1, SLO2, SLO3).

3. Describe the connection between professional development and fidelity of implementation. How is the success of each measured for strategic planning purposes (SLO1, SLO3, SLO4)?

REFLECTION AND APPLICATION

1. Consider the challenges for a school leader in facilitating the implementation of new strategies with fidelity. Why might a lack of fidelity hinder improvement? Why shouldn't teachers be allowed to implement newly learned strategies as they wish?

2. Based on your knowledge of strategic planning, describe three challenges school faculties face in implementing new strategies for teaching and learning and how those challenges might be overcome.

REFERENCES

Dean, C., & Parsley, D. (2010). *Success in sight: Segment 3.1.* McREL.

Fullan, M. (2006). *Turnaround leadership.* Jossey-Bass.

Hanover Research. (2014). *Best practices for school improvement planning.*

LaTurner, J., & Lewis, D. (2013). Managing the improvement of school improvement efforts. *SEDL Insights, 1*(2), 1–6.

Loeb, S., & Plank, D. (2008). Learning what works: Continuous improvement in California's education system. *Policy Analysis for California Education.* https://cepa.stanford.edu/sites/default/files/Learning%20Brief.pdf

Marzano, R. (2011). Art and science of teaching: It's how you use a strategy. *Educational Leadership, 69*(40), 88–89.

Reeves, D. (2006). *The learning leader: How to focus school improvement for better results.* ASCD.

Schmoker, M. (2006). *Results now: How we can achieve unprecedented improvements in teaching and learning.* ASCD.

Sull, D., Homkes, R., & Sull, C. (2015). Why strategy execution unravels—and what to do about it. *Harvard Business Review, 93*(3), 57–66.

Monitoring, Assessment, and Evaluation of Implementation

VIGNETTE

At Anne Smith's school, administrators, the strategic manager, instructional coaches, and teacher leaders working with the implementation process were monitoring classrooms where teachers were initiating the targeted strategies, both to acknowledge teachers' work and to support them in the implementation process. During the first weeks of implementation, there was an intent for the monitoring of personnel, including school leaders and support personnel, to be highly visible.

The monitoring process, which was to take place initially as daily and weekly checks during the initial operationalization, was built into the strategic planning implementation plan. Formal implementation monitoring processes to gather qualitative and quantitative data were established for 30, 60, and again at 90 days. Though the first 30-day review would not provide much data, subsequent reviews with more information would provide more precise data reflecting how the implementation and strategies were working.

In the first week, the strategic manager and implementing teachers held a quick meeting at the end of each day to address implementation issues. The first days had been rocky as newly learned strategies were initiated to use with students; teachers were not yet fluid users. Resources such as on-site (classroom) support (step-by-step review and modeling) were provided when either monitors or teachers were unsure or hesitant about the implementation. The implementation plan called for a gradual release process as teachers felt more confident in the use of targeted strategies; the strategic planning implementation process was to scale up the implementation to include more participants.

Assessment and evaluation in the first stages of implementation were established as pieces of the implementation plan, more qualitative data; teachers used short, end-of-day meetings to provide experiential and anecdotal qualitative data. As the process continued and implementation became the norm, assessments provided initial data; however, initial data did not provide enough information to make evaluative judgements.

LEARNING OUTCOMES

After reading this chapter, the learner should be able to do the following:

1. Define the key words
2. Discuss the process of monitoring
3. Discuss the types of data to be collected when monitoring
4. Discuss monitoring processes
5. Discuss monitoring tools and procedures
6. Discuss analysis

KEY WORDS

Monitoring

Evaluation

Results-based monitoring

Outside evaluator

Bias

Monitoring tools

Process monitoring

INTRODUCTION

In strategic planning, **monitoring** is the systematic process of collecting and examining results. Monitoring focuses on the results-based goals and objectives established in the implementation planning process. Monitoring looks both at the process as a whole as well as the relevant pieces making up the whole. The monitoring process is not a casual process; monitoring by leaders, the strategic manager, and support personnel is critical to the success of the implementation process.

Monitoring focuses on the strategies chosen for implementation to improve student achievement (Rohm, 2008). Monitoring is the responsibility of those who are overseeing the process. A mandatory planned process in which details about who will monitor, how often and when, what kind of data will be collected, how data will be analyzed, and how it will be reported are established prior to the strategy implementation.

Monitoring systems need to be established; monitoring is necessary to compare planned results versus actual results, which allow **evaluation** to judge if short-term and, eventually, long-term goals are met. In particular, collection of assessment data provides indication of progress. Thus, school leaders and teacher implementers as monitors are able to make informed decisions about the effectiveness of the implementation strategies as well as the need for follow-up and support in the implementation process (Reeves, 2007).

MONITORING

Results-based monitoring is keyed to collect and identify growth or lack of growth needed to meet targeted student learning objectives. This key process necessitates the establishment of quality control. Data collection activities need to detail who is responsible for data collection methods, who is responsible for how data are analyzed, and how data are reported. As part of quality control, clarifying roles and responsibilities is necessary to ensure that data is trustworthy and credible (Harnack & Seebaum, 2017).

Organizational capacity for monitoring is an issue. As part of the implementation and monitoring process, consideration needs to include establishing the capacity of personnel working with the implementation to monitor implementation. Building monitoring capacity needs to take place at the same time goals and objectives are established. Along with building capacity for teachers with the use of implementation strategies, implementers, overseers, and monitors of the process need to have the skills to determine if strategies are being implemented with fidelity (Frey, 2018). Therefore, building the capacity of all personnel involved in the implementation both to self-monitor and observe and to make reliable judgements about the process needs to be included both as a part of professional development and the implementation process.

THE ROLE OF THE STRATEGIC MANAGER

During the implementation process, the strategic manager needs to be established for oversight. Oversight responsibilities include the ability to objectively consider data to assess the implementation process as well as the fidelity of the implementation—the use of strategies, the frequency of use, and if the strategies are being implemented and implemented with fidelity. Without monitoring if the implementation process is working, implementation outcomes may lead to unintended results.

Poor planning for monitoring; inadequate processes for follow-up, support, and feedback; as well as inconsistent and systematic observation of implementation will not promote success (Patrick et al., 2016). For accountability purposes, agreement on the methods of monitoring need to be established and reaffirmed prior to implementation being initiated, again once implementation is in process, and as initial monitoring processes begin to provide evaluative data. The methods to be used and types of information to be reported are as important as the analysis processes and how the outcomes are to be reported. Evaluative data has to be reported contextually in terms of meeting targeted outcomes.

Additionally, the formal monitoring process, performance evaluation, may necessitate establishing lines of authority in terms of collecting, analyzing, and reporting data through the use of an **outside evaluator**. One concern is to address **bias**; bias in terms of partiality needs to be addressed as part of the monitoring process. For those who are integrally involved in the strategic planning process as well as implementation, perspectives and points of view may not be as credible as data obtained and analyzed by an outside evaluator (Beach & Lindahl, 2015). An outside evaluator, external to the organization, is an important part of the accountability process. An outside evaluator, working as an educational program evaluator, uses the established performance targets to objectively compare results with expectations, thus legitimizing results for all stakeholders.

DATA

Discussion of monitoring methods includes the need for formal observations of the use of strategy processes in classrooms with students, the use of formative assessments with students, and ultimately summative assessments of teachers' implementation of strategies as well as the use of targeted strategies needed to meet objectives and goals for student achievement. In consideration of the monitoring process, it is important to establish what is needed in terms of the desired evaluative information (ESSA, 2015).

What information will provide the required data? Real-time daily and weekly monitoring should provide data to address the impact of what has taken place in terms of preparing and then executing implementation. Using checklists along with the implementation planning is a key part of the initial monitoring and assessment process. Checklists need to be used by on-site monitors and reviewed by the outside evaluator, who may concurrently use the same checklist for comparative purposes. This process allows monitors to identify and share gaps in implementation. **Monitoring tools** developed with the help of implementing teachers need to reflect agreement on how frequently monitoring takes place, what process strategies are to be monitored, and what methods are to be used to get the data necessary for feedback. Monitoring tools need to be constructed as checklists: digital or pencil/ paper. Monitoring tools need to be constructed to meet the needs of the personnel who are monitoring school leaders and support personnel as well as checklists for self-monitoring by implementing teachers.

Monitoring also tracks implementation progress to see if implementation processes are on track and to ascertain if strategy implementation is taking place within designated timelines (Reeves, 2007). Additionally, monitoring tools provide implementation data on if strategies are implemented or not or require adjustments, improvement or change, or intervention by school leaders. Monitoring processes need to review the implementation process of meeting short-term objectives as well as long-term objectives. Monitors also need to consider the aspects that may be positive or adversely affecting the implementation process and/or student learning.

DATA ANALYSIS

Analysis of data is also an object for discussion. Once leaders and teachers review the findings, evaluation discussion needs to focus on implementation processes as well as gap analysis. How to increase performance and stay on timelines and reviewing projected student outcomes are also discussion topics (Rice, 2017). Baseline data provides a method to track the implementation process and progress toward meeting goals and objectives. Baseline data is also the indicator to determine if timelines are being met. **Process monitoring** is the assessment or evaluation of a program.

Process Monitoring Questions

1. Have the strategies been implemented?
2. Is there fidelity of implementation?
3. Are goals being achieved?
4. Will goals be achieved within established timelines?
5. Are deadlines realistic and achievable?
6. Are improvements warranted?
7. What actions are needed by management?

One of the results of the monitoring process includes presenting the monitoring findings—debriefing teachers in terms of what is occurring, comparing the actual performance to the desired performance.

CONCLUSION

Monitoring, assessment, and evaluation are critical elements to assure that implementation is moving in the right direction. What is going to be implemented, how it is implemented, as well as assessment, monitoring, and evaluation of the implementation process need to be established—routine processes. Monitoring is the systematic process of collecting data on a process and focuses on the indicators established in the monitoring protocol to ascertain results. Like monitoring, assessment, in terms of analysis of data, needs to be decided before the implementation process. Data is needed to guide, coordinate, and implement; assess the effectiveness; identify areas for improvement; and ensure accountability. Evaluation is the last critical step in the implementation process.

IMPLICATIONS FOR SCHOOL LEADERS

School leaders responsible for inculcating change processes in schools have to be intrepid leaders. Getting teachers and stakeholders to buy into the process is key. Much time is required to establish the needs assessment process; the needs assessment results provide key elements to obtaining agreement about what needs to be done to improve student performance.

Moving from professional development to the actual implementation is a different challenge. While support and encouragement from school leaders is helpful, it still takes teachers as everyday implementers to implement newly learned strategies. There will be inevitable discouragement when implementation does not roll out smoothly.

Monitors will report diffident use of strategies with some implementers; not every teacher will be a cheerleader for change. Establishing expectations in terms of what is necessary provides constant challenges in terms of leadership. Teacher statements about the change process in terms of willingness to push through the early stages until seeing success can falter; however, it is the school leader's responsibility to monitor the process, use evaluative data to judge the process, and make evaluations in terms of teacher performance.

The educational responsibility of being a school leader is not easy and remains challenging. As the positive influencer in the implementation process, the leader has both external responsibilities for the district and internal responsibilities to the school to make evaluative observations for teacher implementers struggling with the implementation processes.

FOLLOW-UP ON VIGNETTE

During the first weeks of implementing targeted strategies, school leaders, the strategic manager, instructional coaches, and teacher leaders were involved in the process of monitoring implementation. Snapshot checks of implementation on a daily basis moved to weekly checks as initial implementation of targeted strategies became routine. For school-based personnel, the monitoring process changed from an unusual influx of observers to the new norm of monitors frequently coming into classrooms to observe both the teacher and the students.

The initial 30-day review of implementation did not provide much data, and there were hints that more data at the 60-day monitoring cycle would show progress in meeting goals and objectives. There were some teachers who had not been as quick to implement the strategies in the implementation process.

It had been established that resources such as on-site (classroom) support (step-by-step review and modeling) were to be provided if teachers were unsure and hesitant. The strategic manager played a key part in monitoring, observing, and providing data and ensuring that support was not just talked about—it was provided. Teachers also were aware that there were strong expectations for them to become better and more fluid users of adopted strategies.

Monitoring took a great deal of time, and administrative leaders were aware that instructional coaches needed to play key roles in working and supporting teachers. To achieve their plan of gradual release so that the school could include more teachers in the process was still a work in progress. There were challenges in meeting timelines; discussions about timelines were constantly considered, yet there was a reluctance with everyone to change established timelines.

The first visit by the outside evaluator to monitor the process was nearing at the end of 90 days, and both leaders and teachers were concerned about the evaluative process and how it might differ from the perspective of those who were participants in the process. However, teachers, leaders, and stakeholders wanted to know if their cautious optimism about the process and predicted outcomes were going to be objectively validated.

REFLECTION

Strategic planners (leaders, teachers, and stakeholders) want to be successful in terms of what the needs assessment reflects in terms of what needs to change. Putting the process on paper is one step; implementation is not so easy. For school leaders, one of the necessities is to establish expectations for definitive processes needed for change. Providing the impetus for change is also important, but planning and inculcating change is not an easy process with faculties weary of year-to-year mandates for change. Initiative fatigue is an issue when top-down mandates force changes with little time for planning, professional development, implementation, monitoring, and evaluation, usually tied to punitive measures.

Every year teachers reviewed student performance; every year teachers planned to improve student performance. The difference in this past year was the inclusion of stakeholders, not just teachers and students but those in the community who had vested interests in student achievement outcomes in the process of planning to make advances in performance. Still, just providing the process for making change was a tenuous one. Teachers actually had to change and implement new teaching processes; administrators had to monitor the process and ensure that strategy processes were implemented and teachers were provided the support needed for implementation. Change actually had to take place, and it needed to happen within the timelines that were established.

Implementation processes included time for teachers to work together to implement the strategies that were designed and to support one another in learning the strategies. The professional development processes had taken place, planning for strategy implementation had taken place, and now the focus was on monitoring the process to ensure that it was in place.

CHAPTER 8 QUESTIONS

1. Planned results are often different than the real results obtained when implementing a strategic plan. Why is results-based monitoring beneficial when monitoring progress and evaluating the continuous improvement (SLO1, SLO2, SLO4)?
2. Identify five monitoring tools; describe what type of data is provided and how the information will be applied to the monitoring and evaluation process of the strategic plan (SLO1, SLO2, SLO3, SLO5).
3. The use of an outside evaluator decreases the bias of monitoring and evaluating continuous improvement. As the school leader, prepare a presentation to stakeholders where an outside evaluator's evaluation is different than the leadership team's. Explain the analysis of data used, the process used to monitor improvement, and adjustments to procedures in the strategic plan (SLO1, SLO3, SLO4, SLO6).

REFLECTION AND APPLICATION

1. Reflect on the types of monitoring processes used in your school site. Provide two examples of how monitoring takes place, data is collected and analyzed, and results are examined.

2. Interview two teachers who work at different schools about monitoring processes at their schools. Ask each teacher to share an example of the following: two tools currently used for monitoring student achievement; how the monitoring tools are used; how the data from the monitoring tools are analyzed; and how the results are reported to the teachers who are being monitored.

REFERENCES

Beach, R. H., & Lindahl, R. A. (2015). A discussion of strategic planning as understood through the theory of planning and its relevance to education. *Educational Planning, 22*(2), 5–16.

Every Student Succeeds Act (ESSA) of 2015, P.L. 114-95, S.1177, 114th Cong. (2015).

Frey, B. (Ed.). (2018). *The SAGE encyclopedia of educational research, measurement, and evaluation* (Vols. 1–4). SAGE.

Harnack, J., & Seebaum, M. (2017). *Finding simplicity on the other side of complexity: A strategic planning process streamlines district work and improves the system for all.* McREL International.

Patrick, S., Worthen, M., Frost, D., & Gentz, S. (2016). *Meeting the Every Student Succeeds Act's promise: State policy to support personalized learning.* International Association for K–12 Online Learning (iNACOL).

Reeves, D. (2007). Making strategic planning work. *Educational Leadership, 65*(4), 86–87.

Rice, J. (2017). The disconnect between heralded business concepts and effective school leadership. *Educational Planning, 24*(2), 55–61.

Rohm, H. (2008). *Balanced scorecard.* Balanced Scorecard Institute.

CHAPTER 9

Ongoing Evaluation

VIGNETTE

The leadership team was meeting; early data forecasted success, and data collection cycles verified the early projections; however, there were still ongoing
challenges with scaling up to include more teachers in the implementation cycle.
A major challenge continued to be the need to support and follow up with the
initial teachers and scaling up and following up with support for new implementers. And while most teachers were using the strategies, it was easy to see
lapses in use. Leadership responsibilities still included the necessity to check
and make sure that collaborative planning took place as well as implementation.
Automaticity of use could not be taken for granted.

Because the implementation involved the use of technology, there were
ongoing issues with budgeting and scaling up use. While the district provided
initial support for the implementation, continued district support for purchase
and maintenance of hardware in terms of infrastructure and software were tenuous; there were always other schools with priorities, and since this school was
showing growth in student performance, this school was now not a major focus
for the district. There were discussions about costs for professional development
and support personnel defaulting to the school's budget if the school wanted to
maintain the level of support for teachers.

Yearly budget allocations to the school initially included adding support personnel and faculty to support professional development and follow-up, and the

collaborative planning process needed to keep the implementation successful (Darling-Hammond et al., 2017). Setting aside time in the school day necessitated the addition of faculty to cover classes for collaborative planning times or paying teachers to come in early or stay late to participate in collaborative planning. At the school level, school leaders and teachers were concerned that without financial support, the strategic planning process would be just another initiative, important initially but one that was not so important in terms of budget support now that the implementation process was showing success.

Continual assessment and evaluation were now standard operating procedures with the implementation. While using outside evaluation was important in terms of evaluative capacity to gather data that supported the success of the implementation, using an outside evaluator was another cost factor. While a strategic plan included evaluation in terms of assessment data, it was soon clear in terms of expertise that faculty could carry on with formative normal assessment processes; objective evaluation was necessary to gather multiple perspectives and for decision makers to look at the long-term data.

LEARNING OUTCOMES

After reading this chapter, the learner should be able to do the following:

1. Define the key words
2. Discuss the need to have continuous evaluation processes
3. Discuss the process of continuous evaluation
4. Discuss the analysis process

KEY WORDS

Continuous evaluation   Decision makers
Milestones   Sustainability

INTRODUCTION

A strategic plan is often referred to as a "living plan." In terms of strategic planning for schools, they are often approached in terms of school years; each year school leaders and faculties are required to review their plans and typically change what was established in the previous year based on yearly assessments of student performance. One of the issues with annual evaluation based on student performance scores is that there may be changes that need to be addressed prior to scheduled annual review. Strengths, weaknesses, opportunities, and threats can change within short periods of time. Outside factors may prey on the best-laid plans, necessitating change.

Continuous evaluation of a strategic plan needs to be an established part of the strategic planning process. The evaluation process provides data needed to make short- and longer-term decisions. Strategic plans are established with short-term and long-term goals. Thus, measurement of what is being accomplished, evaluation, has to be continuous to assure that targets are being met. If evaluative data does not provide positive data, it is necessary to revisit the plan to figure out which factors are affecting the progress. Evaluation necessitates reporting data on each of the pieces involved in the plan, and as the plan has multiple parts, the evaluative process has to include measurement of the pieces of the plan as well as provide data to consider the whole picture.

A major piece of strategic planning involves execution. Process monitoring questions become evaluation questions, which need to continually address the implementation pieces.

Evaluation Monitoring Questions

1. Have the strategies been implemented?
2. Is there fidelity of implementation?
3. Are goals being achieved?
4. Will goals be achieved within established timelines?
5. Are deadlines realistic and achievable?
6. Are improvements warranted?
7. What actions need to be taken by management?

At the core is the constant need to assess and evaluate if the implementation is working.

CONTINUOUS EVALUATION

Evaluation necessitates planned, continual assessments to determine effectiveness of the implementation process. Establishing frequent and standardized formative assessment processes is necessary. Using evaluative measures that gather both qualitative and quantitative data is important. Assessment and evaluation of student learning needs to take place constantly. At issue is the necessity to ensure students are mastering learning standards.

Regularity of assessment allows teachers to diagnose learning successes or gaps in the context of meeting learning goals; this process requires comparison of baseline data and newly acquired data. Both informal assessment by classroom teachers and standardized formative assessments provide data for evaluation. The evaluator then makes comparisons to learning targets and provides information for decision making.

DuFour (2004) addressed responsibilities for student performance in terms of four questions:

1. What do students need to know?
2. How will we know they learned it?
3. What do we do when students have not learned what they need to know?
4. What about students who have already reached mastery?

Without assessment and evaluation, it is not possible to address students' learning needs.

Milestones are set up in the implementation process as established dates for processes to take place; milestones in the strategic planning process are keyed to evaluation and used to assess if the implementation processes are on target. Strategic plan evaluation may need to take place in terms of more frequent cycles of evaluation at milestones though not at the depth of quarterly evaluation cycles. School leaders need to check on implementation frequently to ascertain if implementation and targeted strategies to meet increased student performance are taking place. With the need to follow up and support teachers, it is important that in collaborative planning sessions planning for assessment and evaluation are included. The evaluative process needs to be set up in terms of weekly as well as quarterly, biannual, and yearly evaluation.

While the strategic planning overall targeted outcomes need to be addressed in continuous evaluative processes, individual pieces also need evaluation. Data from multiple areas evaluated provide a broader spectrum of multilayered factors underlying the effectiveness of an implementation. Support, especially technical, and follow-up are critical in the process of implementing a strategic plan.

Additional training and professional development to promote the acquisition and use of strategies to use with students is also important. While assessing the actual implementation of the strategies, one additional evaluative factor is the need to provide the support and follow-up necessary to sustain the process of improvement. Effectiveness of the response to requests for support and follow-up are necessary as provisions are tied to financial costs of sustaining an implementation.

Table 9.1 Elements of Continuous Evaluation

	MONITORING	EVALUATIVE METHOD	PERSON RESPONSIBLE	EVALUATION
WHAT NEEDS TO BE CHECKED	Collaborative planning	Document analysis	Strategic manager Outside evaluator	Collaboration and planning data
	Milestones	Comparison of targeted dates to desired outcomes	Strategic manager School leaders	
	Implementation	Checklists	School leaders Strategic manager	Collaborative planning and implementation data
	Support and follow-up	Logs	Strategic manager	Professional development data
METHOD(S)	Walkthroughs	Logs	Strategic manager School leaders	Implementation reports
	Teacher observation	Observation forms	School leaders	Success in implementation
	Scheduled meetings	Agenda, Minutes	School leaders	Reports to strategic planning stakeholders
	Assessments	Formative	Teachers	Assessment reports
FREQUENCY/ TIMING	Daily, weekly, and scheduled benchmarks	Equipment logs	Technology coordinator	Reports on equipment use; software updates
DATA	Logs, observation forms, assessment data	Data and document analysis	School leaders Strategic manager Teachers	Summative student performance data
REPORTS			Outside evaluator	Phased reports: quarterly, biannually, yearly to all stakeholders

Continuous evaluation is the measurement of progress toward both short- and long-term goals, reviewing the key indicators of progress and comparing results (actual versus projected) toward achievement. Results-based monitors are faculty and staff members who make daily, weekly, and scheduled benchmark checks on implementation areas to gather evidence and data. Key **decision makers** need phased data reports to improve the implementation process and to ascertain the effectiveness of the process. One result of results-based monitoring is the ability to provide data about the progress as well as the **sustainability** or continuation of the process.

An outside evaluator is a key element in continuous evaluation as an objective analysis of differing kinds of data is needed. Outside evaluators can work with multiple factors and have the capacity to interpret rigorous data that may be challenging yet are necessary to make determinations of project success. Established methods for evaluation provide evidence of credible, reliable information and take into consideration outside factors or variables that may affect both implementation processes and outcomes. Outside evaluation data is also useful data that provides information at phased points for all stakeholders rather than school leaders and faculty members.

With school leaders needing to be able to make difficult decisions regarding funding and sustainability, it is necessary to have systematic data-gathering processes and evaluation data for decision making processes. Monitoring and evaluation also allow tracking of implementation and effectiveness. School leadership is "second only to classroom teaching as an influence on pupil learning" (Day et al., 2016, p. 222). In terms of strategic planning, this necessitates proactive rather than reactive leadership. Part of the continuing evaluative process is the need to obtain unbiased perspective.

School leaders need to be informed decision makers. Leadership is an action skill, and decision making is necessary as an outcome from the continuous evaluation process. Making data-driven decisions based on the examination of pertinent data, discussing results, and drawing conclusions are part of the cycle of continuous improvement. To ensure data-driven decision making, the evaluation elements must be in place for the evaluative process to be effective. Reports from an outside evaluator provide objective data to determine if a program is successful, if changes are needed, and if an implementation project is ready to be scaled up and/or can be sustained. One of the additional areas of decision making comes with affordability and cost effectiveness of implementation projects. Implementation may be successful but not ultimately sustainable in terms of cost effectiveness.

CONCLUSION

Ultimately, there is no choice about the process of continuous evaluation. Data that provides information about educational achievement is necessary. Informal and formal evaluation allow school leaders to analyze and make decisions in the best interests of students. Evaluative data that addresses how well both instructional targets and milestones are being met answer questions about results and progress.

The purpose of the strategic planning process was to address persistent, pervasive, significant disparities and, ultimately, attainment of students as determined by the established measures of assessment. All actions in the school improvement process and strategic planning are tied to meeting the vision established for all students to be successful.

IMPLICATIONS FOR SCHOOL LEADERS

School leaders want the best for their schools. Moving to the process of strategic planning takes large amounts of time; however, what school leaders saw is that the process changed the view of the school in the community. There were people who had never been participants in school events who now saw themselves as being a part of the movement to improve student performance. Encouraging stakeholders to become a part of the strategic planning had taken a lot of time and a lot of patience for people who ultimately wanted good things for students but might lack an educational background.

There was no easy solution when planning for improvement necessitated in making change. Teachers were resistant, and in the case of this strategic plan, the outcomes for teachers were to learn how to use technology in order to incorporate it in teaching strategies. The professional development process took time, money, and effort. The choice of starting with small numbers of teachers to initiate the process and using collaborative planning as the method to promote the process had worked though some teachers were initially resistant.

One of the outcomes was the need to designate a school administrative member to be the strategic manager of the implementation and monitoring process. Because they were working with multiple grades and subject areas and there was necessity to provide follow-up and support to faculty, someone had to both monitor and continuously make decisions about the process. Ultimately, it was necessary to get an outside evaluator who had the ability and capacity to carry out the evaluation process from an unbiased perspective so that the evaluation was a credible product.

Another major outcome had been the acquisition of knowledge for the school leadership team who thought they knew what they were taking on in terms of committing to a strategic planning process. The school leadership team had learned as much as others working with the process, learning that their involvement was to ensure expectations were established; as school leaders they had to be visible participants, and they needed to be part of the monitoring process. The strategic planning process in a school setting was a process that required participation by all.

FOLLOW-UP ON VIGNETTE

It was a little strange not to be in the throes of implementing a massive project. For the last several school years, there was always a move to scale up the implementation process outlined in the strategic plan goals. Now, as school leaders, they were nearing the end of the time frame of the strategic plan, and though evaluation was still taking place and student improvement goals were always present, there was not as much urgency and pressure to improve student performance.

There was a new norm in the school; teacher expectations were to work collaboratively with planning to use strategies to improve student performance. While initially collaborative planning was strictly targeted to improvement initiatives, the process had morphed to include all areas and subjects taught. There was an expectation by teachers that everyone at this school participated in collaborative planning and was willing to implement the strategies that they worked out in planning.

There were always challenges to train, support, and follow up with new teachers. And there were still teachers who were not willing users; there were those who lapsed in using the targeted strategies. However, it was taken for granted that there would be evaluators in the form of the strategic manager, instructional coaches, and school leaders who would monitor lessons and check classes to see if the implementation was ongoing.

An unexpected result was the reaction from students. Students took note of the process of implementing technology strategies into lessons. As the culture of the school changed and teachers worked with collaborative planning and implemented strategies, students now expected to see teachers working with technology, and they expected teachers to be knowledgeable about the technology. Teachers also wanted more digital technology devices, and they wanted help to learn the technology. Infrastructure in terms of bandwidth was always an issue. Students wanted to learn different digital technologies, and if teachers did not use it when teaching, students did not hesitate to voice their opinions.

Teachers heard administrators voice concerns in strategic planning meetings that there were ongoing issues with budgeting and scaling up use. The district had provided support for the implementation through federal and district monies. Now this school was not a priority school; there were other schools that were now priorities. Teachers were worried that their strategic planning process would become just another initiative that was phased out.

One of the successes is that teachers really liked collaborative planning. In fact, to supplement time that was not so easy to find during the school day, often departments met before or after school to work on planning. In interviewing teachers who wanted to move to the school, one of the questions was about expectations for teachers to participate in collaborative planning before and after school and during the school day. The expectation was voiced, and teacher contracts elaborated the expectations.

The strategic planning process was an accepted part of school culture. Out-of-class teacher discussions were about strategic planning and addressed the fact that the "old one" was running out and that it was time to consider a new strategic plan. Teachers who were on the Strategic Planning Committee discussed possible plans with community stakeholders who saw themselves as participants in the process. The process had been challenging for everyone and had taken a great deal of time, but stakeholders saw themselves as part of the process, part of the new norm for this school.

REFLECTION

School leadership is such a challenge; leading a strategic plan process is even more challenging. With the strategic planning process, once the needs assessment points out what needs to be addressed, planning and implementation processes are immediate outcomes. However, the strategic process had been a return on investment in terms of the improvement of student performance.

One outcome was the recognition of the necessity of school and district leaders to be heavily involved in the strategic planning process. It was obvious from stakeholder and teacher discussions that each felt the school leadership's involvement in the monitoring and evaluation process was integral to success. Participation in the process by school leaders was not one of handing off the process and watching from afar. From the district leadership (in terms of support) as well as in the visibility of district leaders, stakeholders voiced satisfaction about the involvement of all leaders.

CHAPTER 9 QUESTIONS

1. As a process in strategic planning, identify the benefits of short- and long-term evaluations in the continuous evaluations process. What is the school leader's responsibility in these evaluations (SLO1, SLO2)?

2. Evaluations of processes in the strategic plan can take place weekly, quarterly, biannually, and yearly. Explain what milestones are assessed using each timeline of evaluation and how analysis at each timeline impacts continuous improvement (SLO1, SLO2, SLO3).

3. The school leader, as a key decision maker, is responsible for accountability in terms of continuous improvement. How does the school leader quantify and determine the sustainability of processes included in a strategic plan (SLO1, SLO3, SLO4)?

REFLECTION AND APPLICATION

1. Continuous evaluations are necessary to make decisions regarding student academic achievement. How does the evaluation process hold both the school leader and teachers accountable?

2. High-performing school leaders understand that evaluation processes are critical parts of the continuous improvement process. List and explain three ways a high-performing school leader supports the sustainability of the continuous evaluation processes.

REFERENCES

Darling-Hammond, L., Hyler, M. E., & Gardner, M. (2017). *Effective teacher professional development.* Learning Policy Institute.

Day, C., Gu, Q., & Sammons, P. (2016). The impact of leadership on student outcomes: How successful school leaders use transformational and instructional strategies to make a difference. *Educational Administration Quarterly, 52*(2), 221–258. https://doi.org/10.1177/0013161X15616863

DuFour, R. (2004). What is a "professional learning community"? *Educational Leadership, 61*(8), 6–11.

Every Student Succeeds Act (ESSA) of 2015, P.L. 114-95, S.1177, 114th Cong. (2015).

Frey, B. (Ed.). (2018).*The SAGE encyclopedia of educational research, measurement, and evaluation* (Vols. 1–4). SAGE.

Reeves, D. (2007). Making strategic planning work. *Educational Leadership, 65*(4), 86–87.

Rice, J. (2017). The disconnect between heralded business concepts and effective school leadership. *Educational Planning, 24*(2), 55–61.

Rohm, H. (2008). *Balanced scorecard.* Balanced Scorecard Institute.

CHAPTER 10

Conclusion

VIGNETTE

Anne Smith's school leadership team had learned a lot about their community and their school in the process of using the strategic planning process. One of the gains for the school was that participants in the strategic planning process included stakeholders, not just a small number of parents and a few teachers. For the first time since Anne had been a school leader she had community stakeholders who were actively working with the school. In fact, their input facilitated more engagement from students who saw stakeholders as school participants. Community stakeholders were involved in school activities, and students knew many of them by name.

Another part of the process was the increased interest from parents who reflected diverse perspectives. Anne's school had changed a great deal in the past 10 years, and in the time since the strategic planning process had been underway, student demographics continued to change. Students were often English language learners (ELL) and more students qualified for free and reduced lunches. Parents who were once hesitant to visit and participate in activities participated more actively now. As part of the strategic planning process, school leaders and teachers had been taking second language lessons, and though their skills were tentative, just making the effort to address parents in their first language elicited better responses. Most of the signage in the school and all of the information about school events were now published in two or more languages.

Stakeholders were welcoming now; once hesitant as they were not able to contribute monetarily to school causes, they were willing to post information at business sites and to welcome students to work part-time positions in the community. Anne also had better working relationships with governmental and nongovernmental agencies who were now sometime sponsors of things they needed to promote; they were more collaborative and supportive in planning events.

Going through the strategic planning process and implementing the recommended strategies had produced positive changes in student performance. There were still achievement gaps in expected outcomes; however, there were established processes to address what happened when students did not learn as they were expected to. Students with learning gaps were addressed through intervention programs.

There were also students who had really tapped into the benefits of being able to access the information and focus on processes that met their learning needs. Higher performing students were able to integrate into programs that propelled them on to making greater progress in their educational careers. Some students were able to move into dual enrollment plans, which allowed them to gain college credits.

LEARNING OUTCOMES

After reading this chapter, the learner should be able to do the following:

1. Define substantive involvement in terms of stakeholders
2. Discuss gap analysis
3. Discuss priorities in terms of school improvement
4. Discuss an evaluation final report

KEY WORDS

Substantive involvement
Collective commitment

Gap analysis
Return on investment

INTRODUCTION

Today's schools and school systems must tackle complex and evolving demands. Educators face myriad challenges, all of which demand that schools address continuous improvement (Reeves, 2007). Strategic planning provides a systematic method to use for decision-making purposes in terms of continuous school improvement mandates, usually targeting improving student performance.

USE OF STRATEGIC PLANNING

Strategic planning has been used by school systems since the 1980s (Beach & Lindahl, 2007, 2015). Today, schools are governed by the Every Student Succeeds Act (ESSA, 2015), which requires a systemic planning process. ESSA guidance, unlike No Child Left Behind (2001) provides more time for a planning process; strategic planning as a systemic process is not a quick process. The intent is ESSA funding be used to implement what stakeholders have determined to be the top priorities for improving student performance.

One key change was ESSA language mandating stakeholder involvement in the process of systemic planning; ESSA provisions required the **substantive involvement** of all stakeholders and documentation of their involvement in the planning process. Based on the transfer of responsibility from federal mandates to local-level decision-making processes, ESSA guidance promoted the need for a systemic planning process that encouraged schools to develop their own mission (purpose), vision (direction), needs assessment (improvement focus), strategies (actions to reach improvement goals), processes (to implement strategies), monitoring (accountability), and evaluation (accountability and performance indicators). Strategic planning is a cyclical process. Key components include the following:

- Identification of needs
- Analysis of data
- Prioritizing achievable goals and objectives
- Building capacity for stakeholders
- Choosing strategies to reach objectives
- Implementation
- Monitoring and evaluation
- Reevaluation for ongoing continuous improvement

NEEDS ASSESSMENT

As part of ESSA requirements and the strategic planning process, a needs assessment is promoted as a method to conduct a systemic analysis of what exists. In this case, the needs assessment is focused on the school with the intent to address underlying causes of poor student performance. Stakeholders representing school leaders, teachers, parents, and students are participants both in the organization as well as participants in the needs assessment process; there is a **collective commitment** to work toward increased student performance. The purpose for the needs assessment is to identify differences between current performance and desired performance, sometimes referred to as **gap analysis**. The needs assessment also identifies strengths as well as areas needed for improvement and information about needed resources. Finally, data from the needs assessment analysis provides information necessary to establish priorities and milestones in terms of timelines.

Student performance provided the impetus to contemplate a change process in terms of systemic strategic planning. The ultimate goal of the strategic planning process was to establish a systematic process to tackle the processes school leaders and faculty needed to address, to determine supports and resources, and to develop milestones to track student performance (Chan, 2010).

This strategic plan was intended to address one school and to focus on classroom-level data to support improved student performance (Harnack & Seebaum, 2017). Thus, the strategic planning needs assessment process provided a method to obtain data that supported rationale for change, proposed areas for change, and recommended strategies to be used to promote growth in student performance.

Moving from the outcomes of the assessment of needs to the implementation of recommended strategies to promote change were major accomplishments. Data from the needs assessment recommended professional development to provide teachers with the capacity to implement strategies with targeted student populations, ultimately scaling up implementation of recommended strategies to the entire faculty. Throughout the entire process there was an emphasis on assessment, monitoring and gathering formative and summative data, evaluating through an analysis of data, and comparing the data to context embedded outcomes (Beach & Lindahl, 2007, 2015).

The adoption of a strategic planning process was driven by the recognition that without all stakeholders' buy-in using targeted strategies to change student performance there might be little **return on investment**. Return on investment for the strategic planning process was to gain the best possible growth in student performance.

For this strategic planning process, there was district support with funding for professional development, personnel, and technology to support the process. Initially, costs were not a concern because the needs were critical. With success and with increase in performance by the targeted students, district priorities changed, targeting different schools and different populations. There was no longer an urgency to do whatever was necessary to promote change at this school.

FINAL EVALUATION REPORT

An outside evaluator can produce a final report that is a summation of the strategic planning process and its successes and concerns. Continuous evaluation data reported by the outside evaluator provides data in terms of stakeholder involvement, needs assessment outcomes, professional development, follow-up and support, and implementation of targeted strategies and assessment data that reported productivity in terms of student performance levels. The data are delivered in context of the instructional performance goals established for the strategic plan implementation, tying the monetary investment to the student performance outcomes.

Ultimately, the final evaluation report stated the strategic planning process had multiple strengths and continuing concerns.

Strengths

1. The strategic planning process garnered stakeholders as participatory members of the school community; stakeholders include teachers, school leaders, students, parents, state agencies, nonprofit and civic organizations, businesses, and education advocacy groups.
2. Based on the needs assessment data, stakeholders, school leaders, and teachers agreed about strategies needed to promote improvement in student performance and desired outcomes.
3. Professional development, follow-up, support, and the implementation of collaborative planning allowed teachers to implement the use of targeted strategies.
4. The school was able to scale up a small phased-in implementation into a school-wide implementation.
5. The collective commitment of all stakeholders, leaders, teachers, parents, students, and community members changed the school culture.

Concerns

1. Sustaining the level of funding needed at this school as student performance improved was no longer a priority target for district funding.
2. Continuing the current level of support for professional development and collaborative planning was costly, and the individual school budget allocation amounts suggested lack of district funds could affect the processes implemented to achieve better student performance.
3. District leaders suggested that while student performance improved, less costly methods might be used to improve student performance.
4. There were data that suggested student improvement gains were leveling off and no longer climbing; different methods of intervention might be warranted.

5. Collective commitment had changed the school culture; however, sustaining and/or renewing the strategic planning process was necessary.

6. School leaders were concerned that if funding was cut stakeholders would become less involved as they did not see the same level of commitment from the district to the school.

7. Teachers who were hearing about district-level funding concerns expressed that, once again, this was just "another school initiative" and their hard work would not be respected for successes.

8. Students had high expectations for strategies that were being used in classes; students expected to see teachers use technology and to be able to use technology in their work.

CONCLUSION

There were issues with funding for the upcoming year. District funds and federal funds were targeted both to supporting schools with lower socioeconomic populations: schools with increasing numbers of English language learners, and students who were not meeting expected performance outcomes. While the district intent was to support the school as much as possible, growth in student performance as compared to other schools in the district necessitated revisiting how funds were to be allocated. There were schools with students who did not have as high a performance, and it was necessary to consider changing funding allocations.

No one at the district level considered the strategic planning process as just another initiative; the process had been powerful in terms of changing a school culture to one of both higher expectations and higher student performance. However, strategic planning took time, and there was a push to move as swiftly as possible to address learning issues at other schools. There would ultimately be a reduction in the monetary resources at this school in order to support another school's need to better student academic performance.

IMPLICATIONS FOR SCHOOL LEADERS

The strategic planning process was a return on investment in terms of leadership, teaching, stakeholder involvement, and success for improving student performance outcomes. One outcome was participant acknowledgment of the substantial impact of community and stakeholders' recognition of all the factors that influenced student success and the need for commitment from all stakeholders.

Inevitably, there were still areas for concern. The outside evaluator's final report had denoted areas of success along with a long list of concerns that provided conversation about establishing priorities for further work and the need to revisit the strategic planning process.

At the district level, conversation about strategic planning was focused on the return of investment indicators of the outcomes in terms of dollars spent toward increasing student performance and efficiency in terms of use of the monies. Part of the conversation about return on investment was that there was no way to measure outcomes in terms of long-term effects on student success. Because the strategic planning process ultimately increased student performance, there was no way to make a comparison of what might have happened to students had the strategic planning process not taken place.

Finally, there was already discussion from district leaders with school leaders about how the strategic planning process might be modified or improved in terms of time and money. School leaders felt that one issue with modifying the process would inevitably affect the ability to attract community stakeholders to participate, and because the strategic planning process was focused both on the process as well as the product, modifying the process might inhibit success.

FOLLOW-UP ON VIGNETTE

One long-term outcome of the strategic planning process was the recognition from different types of stakeholders about the multifaceted pieces that were part of the educational process in the community. Another outcome was the change in school culture; there were high expectations for students in terms of performance outcomes, and students were taking a bigger interest in options for their long-term career success by participating in dual enrollment options. Parents were extremely interested in dual enrollment as this option provided access to postsecondary education programs as well as tuition for the costs of classes.

There were more diverse students in the school; many of the students were English language learners, and increases in numbers of students who were on free and reduced lunch status continued. However, parents were participating in more activities as leaders and teachers were trying to acquire second language skills, part of the commitment that had become a part of the strategic planning process. There were also more established relationships with local and state governmental agencies that supported parents and students and better collaboration and planning in terms of addressing community and school needs. Stakeholders participating in the strategic planning process had learned a great deal about themselves, the students, and the possibilities for the future.

REFLECTION

This strategic planning process had many successes; some strategic planning processes are not as successful. Many community members and teachers are reluctant to recognize the need for change and to participate in change processes. Some school districts are unwilling to allocate the time necessary for the strategic planning process.

Under No Child Left Behind, mandates were pushed to schools without consideration of all the factors that affected the ability of the school to increase the performance of all students within a 9-month timeline. Underlying causes could not be addressed in terms of student performance.

While ESSA guidelines still push for increased performance, there is a recognition of the need for a systemic and longer-term process for planning and implementation in order to address both underlying causes of underperformance and long-term issues.

Strategic planning provides a method for systemic change; systematic planning and implementation provide methods to address the needs of schools and school populations while increasing the ability to interact and work with community stakeholders. There is no one correct method of strategic planning; it needs to meet the needs of the users; however, strategic planning does provide a template for a process that can be used to promote success in schools and communities by targeting strategies needed to increase student performance.

CHAPTER 10 QUESTIONS

1. Explain how substantive involvement is essential to prioritizing components addressed in the school improvement process (SLO1, SLO2).
2. Describe ways to increase the collective commitment from stakeholders to best address the needs determined from a gap analysis. How can all stakeholders understand the strategies, procedures, and evaluations outlined in the strategic plan (SLO1, SLO2, SLO3)?
3. Evaluating continuous improvement is an essential step in strategic planning. Compare how a final report might be different from the lens of the school leader, a community stakeholder, and an outside evaluator (SLO1, SLO4).

REFLECTION AND APPLICATION

1. The complexity of the school leader's role has evolved and is challenging. In today's world, school administrators need to be highly committed and willing to deal with the social and emotional issues surrounding students, teachers, and communities. Why do you want to be a school leader?

2. Today's school leaders need a wide variety of competencies. Interview your school administrator and ask for information about how the local district prepares and supports school administrators to ensure continuous school improvement.

REFERENCES

Beach, R. H., & Lindahl, R. A. (2007). The role of planning in the school improvement process. *Educational Planning*, 16(2), 19–43.

Beach, R. H., & Lindahl, R. A. (2015). A discussion of strategic planning as understood through the theory of planning and its relevance to education. *Educational Planning*, 22(2), 5–16.

Chan, T. C. (2010). The implications of symbols in educational planning: 2009–2010 presidential address. *Educational Planning*, 19(2), 1–7.

Every Child Succeeds Act (ESSA), P.L. 114-95, S.1177, 114th Cong. (2015).

Harnack, J., & Seebaum, M. (2017). *Finding simplicity on the other side of complexity: A strategic planning process streamlines district work and improves the system for all.* McREL International.

No Child Left Behind Act of 2001, P.L. 107-110, 20 U.S.C. § 6319 (2002).

Reeves, D. (2007). Making strategic planning work. *Educational Leadership*, 65(4), 86–87.

ADDITIONAL RESOURCES

Allison, M., & Kaye, J. (2015). *Strategic planning for nonprofit organizations: A practical guide and workbook* (2nd ed.). Wiley.

American Institute for Research and The National Association of Elementary School Principals. (2017). *Principals' action plan for the Every Student Succeeds Act: Providing all students with a well-rounded and complete education.*

Batel, S., Sargrad, S., & Jimenez, L. (2016). *Innovation in accountability: Designing systems to support school quality and student success.* Center for American Progress.

Bryson, J. M., & Alston, F. K. (2011). *Creating your strategic plan: A workbook for public and nonprofit organizations.* Jossey-Bass.

Bryson, J. (2011). *Strategic planning for public and nonprofit organizations* (4th ed.). Jossey-Bass.

Bryson, J. M. (2011). *Strategic planning for public and nonprofit organizations: A guide to strengthening and sustaining organizational achievement* (Vol. 1). Wiley.

Chenoweth, K. (2016). ESSA offers changes that can continue learning gains. *Phi Delta Kappan, 97*(8), 38–42. https://doi.org/10.1177/0031721716647017

Hanover Research. (2014). *Best practices for school improvement planning.*

Kaufman, R. A., & Herman, J. J. (1991). *Strategic planning in education: Rethinking, restructure, revitalizing.* Technomic.

Rohm, H. (2008). *Balanced scorecard.* Balanced Scorecard Institute.

Schanzenbach, D. W., Bauer, L., & Mumford, M. (2016). *Lessons for broadening school accountability under the Every Student Succeeds Act.* Brookings Institute.

Steiner, G. A. (2010). *Strategic planning.* Simon & Schuster.

Weiss, J., & McGuinn, P. (2016). States as change agents under ESSA. *Phi Delta Kappan, 97*(8), 28–33. https://doi.org/10.1177/0031721716647015

SWOT Case Study

A case study in educational leadership provides a narrative that presents information to be considered by school leader candidates to represent multiple perspectives. Case studies offer background information about a subject from a school- or district-based context without offering outcomes.

Case studies are often problem based; this forces the school leader candidate to consider actions or decisions and to make recommendations. Case studies represent multiple school settings and situations that often cause challenges for school leaders because there are clear right or wrong answers. Analysis and decision making become the responsibility of the school leader candidate.

SWOT ANALYSIS CASE STUDY STUDENT LEARNING OUTCOMES

1. Students will utilize the information provided in the case study background information. School leader candidates will select processes to obtain information about potential school and district problems, recognize multiple internal and external influences and perspectives about education in the school and district, and apply problem-solving and decision-making processes such as those faced by school leaders.
2. Students will conduct a SWOT analysis using the questions provided for the case study with a sample stakeholder committee.
3. Students will evaluate the information obtained in SWOT interviews and the analysis of interview information from the perspective of a school leader.
4. Students will review the information provided from the analysis and construct some generalizations about the information obtained.
5. Students will consider how the information obtained might apply to their own school or district.
6. Students will infer how the ideas, concepts, and perspectives generalize to other schools in the region.
7. Students will create a briefing paper using data obtained from the SWOT case study background information.

SWOT CASE STUDY BACKGROUND INFORMATION

WHAT IS A PRINCIPAL TO DO?

Mirah Stewart walked down the hall of Springfield Middle School headed to the principal's office. Mirah was beginning her 2nd year as an assistant principal at the school. Although she had learned a great deal during her 1st year, she could only surmise that year 2 would be much more learning. In fact, she was on the way to meet Dr. Seneca, her principal who wanted to talk to Mirah about her new assignment: guiding and directing the Continuous School Improvement Team.

Mirah knew little about the team, what they did, or what was expected of her. Dr. Seneca wanted to discuss the use of SWOT analysis as a way to collect and analyze data to make the school improvement plan more functional, accurate, and encompassing of faculty and community input. Mirah sighed and walked into Dr. Seneca's office knowing that this was going to be a tremendous amount of work but also hoping that this would be a great learning experience. What does the principal want to know? Why has the principal asked her to work on this task? What does she need to know? Where does she begin? And, ultimately, how will the information she obtains work with continuous school improvement processes?

What Is SWOT?

SWOT stands for strengths, weaknesses, opportunities, and threats. A SWOT analysis is a strategic tool used to shape the success of a school. SWOT data provide perspectives for the school about what it can and cannot do both internally and externally, detailing how the school can accomplish its goals and what stands in its way. SWOT analysis is a strategic planning technique that provides assessment tools for schools to analyze their strengths, weaknesses, opportunities, and threats, hence the abbreviation SWOT (Pickton & Wright, 1998). By identifying core strengths, weaknesses, opportunities, and threats, the school leader can focus on fact-based analysis, fresh perspectives, and new ideas to improve the operations of the school and enhance its standing in the community. A SWOT analysis works best when diverse groups or voices within the school are free to provide realistic data and information, share ideas, and openly discuss the elements of the SWOT (Pahl & Richter, 2007).

What Are the Elements of SWOT?

Strengths describe what the school personnel perceive to be the factors that make the school a success. At what things does the school excell and what separates it from others? For example, the school may have an outstanding technology program, have an outstanding record with student achievement, have excellent parental support, or have students who are very successful in attracting college scholarships. A good technique is to turn the perspective around and ask what others might see as your strengths.

Weaknesses are those elements that prevent the school from performing at its optimum level. These are areas where the school needs to improve levels of student academic achievement: higher than average faculty turnover, high levels of student disruptive behavior, poor rating on assessments, and less than satisfactory results for student achievement. Weaknesses are intrinsic features of the school and so focus on people, resources, systems, and procedures. Participating in a SWOT analysis provides a time for critical self-analysis of the school.

Opportunities refer to favorable external factors that could give a school addition resources to make it a more effective educational institution. For example, a new housing subdivision could give the school new students or more students to generate more funding. A new factory could be moving to the area to increase the tax base for education. Opportunities require consideration of what might happen in the future. Spotting and exploiting opportunities can make a huge difference to your school. SWOT analysis also provides options to look for potential changes in government policy at the state or federal level, particularly funding changes. Changes in social patterns, population profiles, and business growth can be opportunities.

Threats refer to factors with the potential to harm the school. For example, businesses could be closing or moving from the area. A new private school could be opening, which could create competition. Bad press over some student or faculty misstep could create a public relations problem. Poor student achievement could create a loss of public support. Considering the threats allows stakeholders to be more knowledgeable about challenges the school faces as quality standards or specifications or regulations are changing. Evolving technology is an ever-present threat as well as an opportunity.

Advantages of SWOT Analysis

A SWOT analysis is a great way to organize and create discussions in faculty, parental, or community stakeholder meetings. It can be a powerful experience to have everyone in the room discuss the school's core strengths and weaknesses and then define the opportunities and threats and, finally, brainstorming ideas.

Oftentimes, the SWOT analysis that school leaders envision before a meeting changes to reflect factors of which the leaders were unaware and would never have captured if not for stakeholder input.

A school can use a SWOT analysis for faculty or community stakeholder meetings to address emerging concerns from school-based grade-level meetings or department meetings. A SWOT analysis can come in the form of brainstorming or self-assessment activities. In order for a SWOT analysis to work, there must be an open atmosphere where everyone is allowed to contribute with their own ideas. A SWOT analysis tends to look deeply within a school to analyze its internal potential (Clardy, 2013).

Analysis of SWOT

Users often go through a SWOT exercise to identify the things they do well and to analyze processes that could lead to difficulty. The strengths and weaknesses are internal characteristics—ones that can be controlled and/or changed, often easily and from the inside. The strengths outline how the school excels and may include location, technology, employees, great parental support, or great students. A school's weaknesses prevent it from performing to its fullest potential. Lack of funding, workforce turnover, and a lack of resources are all examples of weaknesses.

External factors include opportunities and threats, which may not necessarily be easy to contain. The opportunities a school has are the favorable factors, which give it an edge over other schools. Threats, on the other hand, are external factors that can hinder a school's abilities. The purpose of performing a SWOT is to reveal positive forces that work together and potential problems that need to be recognized and possibly addressed (Sarsby, 2016). An examination of external factors may also need a PESTLE analysis.

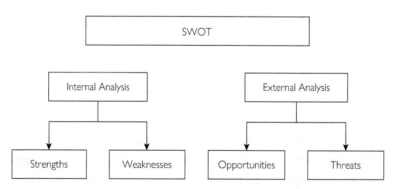

Figure A.1 SWOT Analysis Elements

Procedures for Conducting a SWOT Analysis

1. Designate a leader who has good group process skills and who can keep things moving and on track.
2. Use an electronic device to record meetings and stakeholder information.
3. Introduce the SWOT method and its purpose. This can be as simple as asking, "Where are we? Where can we go?"
4. Depending on the nature of the group, have all participants introduce themselves. Then divide into smaller groups. If the meeting draws several groups of stakeholders together, make sure to mix the small groups to get a range of perspectives, and give them a chance to introduce themselves. The size of these depends on the size of the entire group; breakout groups can range from 3 to 10. If the size gets much larger, some members may not participate.
5. Have each group designate a recorder and provide each with an electronic device. Direct them to create a SWOT analysis in the chosen format.
6. Give the groups 20–30 minutes to brainstorm and fill out their own strengths, weakness, opportunities, and threats chart for your program, initiative, or effort. Encourage participants not to rule out any ideas at this stage or the next.
7. Remind participants the way to have a good idea is to have lots of ideas. Refinement can come later. In this way, the SWOT analysis also supports valuable discussion within groups.
8. Once a list has been generated, it helps to refine it to the best 10 or fewer points so that the analysis can be truly helpful.
9. Reconvene the group at an agreed-on time to share results. Gather information from the groups, recording their suggestions to collect and organize the differing groups' ideas and perceptions.
10. Proceed in SWOT order, recording strengths first, weaknesses second, and so on.
11. Ask one group at a time to report.
12. Discuss and record the results.
13. Prepare a written summary of the SWOT analysis to share with participants for continued use in planning and implementation.
14. The SWOT process can be used with a variety of groups related to the school to collect valuable data and build support for the process.

Why Use a SWOT Analysis?

SWOT analysis equips school leaders with an insightful framework for eliminating issues in a systematic manner that can influence the condition of school and education, including formulation of various strategies and their selection. The analysis presents information from different perspectives about the internal and external environment. This helps in comparing external opportunities and threats with internal strengths and weaknesses to help choose the best strategy (Ghazinoory et al., 2011). Every school has its strengths, weakness, opportunities, and threats. The SWOT analysis acts as a guide for school leaders to determine the position of where the school stands relative to ESSA best practices to help identify the strategy under consideration. SWOT analysis helps the school leader develop continuous school improvement processes that are most advantageous.

The SWOT process is a type of focus group that may be used to analyze ideas, concepts, and institutions and to solve various problems. This process deals with both external and internal factors and can be carried out in two basic ways. The external factors are represented by various threats and opportunities, while the two internal factors are weaknesses and strengths. You may choose to brainstorm strengths and weaknesses first, though it is also popular to begin by identifying opportunities and threats. It is then possible to examine your strengths and weaknesses while keeping in mind specific opportunities and threats faced by your school.

A SWOT analysis highlights and expands strengths. It minimizes or even erases weaknesses. It allows for the creation of opportunities. And it identifies threats to prevent emerging issues. It's a framework to understand the present and future situation of your school (Saitis & Saiti, 2018). And all it takes to complete is time.

A SWOT analysis enables school leaders to understand their school's strengths, weaknesses, opportunities, and threats. Threats include the failure to plan for some of the more obvious circumstances. While it impossible to plan for every scenario, the more common ones should be thought about, discussed, and debated.

SWOT and School Improvement Planning

In today's world almost every school must develop and implement a school improvement plan, sometimes with more than one variety of constituents. A SWOT analysis is an ideal tool for school leaders and faculty to use to determine the most critical focus for school improvement. It also provides validity to the process that can be used for documentation. The SWOT analysis helps identify existing practices in the school, gaps in services, and needs for service improvement. Using a SWOT analysis, school leaders can also become better prepared to face the new challenges and new approaches to learning and teaching brought by technology and new teaching methods, which lead to school improvement (Gurel & Tat, 2017).

CONCLUSIONS

1. SWOT analysis is an invaluable tool for school leaders; planning is vitally important in improving the school.
2. SWOT formalizes the opportunity for school faculty, staff, and stakeholders to take an active role in the school planning process.
3. SWOT gives school leaders insight that might not be obtained in any other way, particularly from community stakeholders.
4. SWOT is an easy tool to use for school improvement that provides great insight and validity.
5. SWOT analysis provides a road map for school leaders to clearly articulate the plan for continued improvement in an era of increased accountability and uncertainty.
6. SWOT analysis is an analytical tool utilized by school leaders to ascertain relevant strategies needed for the school to achieve continuous school improvement.

SCHOOL LEADER CANDIDATE ASSIGNMENTS

- Review the information in the background information.
- Assemble a mock stakeholder community to participate in a SWOT.
- Conduct the SWOT with the community members.
- Analyze the data from the SWOT.
- Assemble and present the findings from the SWOT.
- Prepare a briefing paper on the SWOT, processes, findings, and implications for school leaders.

Procedures to Complete Assignments

1. Review the information provided in the case study background information.
2. Reread the information in the chapter to evaluate the types of information needed in SWOT to construct a committee of stakeholders.
3. Establish a stakeholder committee. The stakeholder committee should be composed of a minimum of five and a maximum of 10 people. School leader candidates may consult with stakeholders through virtual mediums through interviews or surveys. Stakeholder representatives should include, if possible, three teachers, one school leader, one parent, and at least one community member. No committee member should be identified by any personal information.

4. Conduct a SWOT with the committee members to obtain information about potential school and/or district problems, identify multiple internal and external influences and perspectives about education in the school and district, and apply problem-solving and decision-making processes such as those faced by school leaders.

5. Evaluate the information obtained in SWOT interviews or surveys and analyze data obtained from the perspective of a school leader.

6. Assess the findings to construct some generalizations about the information obtained.

7. Predict how the information obtained might apply to student's own school or district.

8. Infer how the ideas, concepts, and perspectives generalize to other schools in the region.

9. Create a briefing paper using data obtained from the SWOT case study background Information.

SWOT ANALYSIS BRIEFING PAPER RUBRIC

STUDENT'S NAME
Briefing Paper Rubric (Maximum of Eight Pages*) 100 Points

Write a short paper (five APA-style pages) based on the topic: SWOT analysis.

There are six required sections in the briefing paper (Introduction, Background Information and Literature Review, Methodology and Data Analysis, Findings, Implications for School Leaders, References).

- Each should be labeled. Designated sections are to be written in third person.
- Two sections (Findings and Implications) can be written in first person as school leader candidates are addressing the issue from their base of knowledge.

Introduction (to the topic) (third person) (10 points)

Include discussion on the following questions in the introduction of the briefing paper:
   (a) Introduce the topic
   (b) Discuss the need for a school leader to obtain the information found in a SWOT analysis

Background Information and Literature Review (third person) (15 points)

Five peer-reviewed journal articles, not less than 5 years old, should be used to provide supportive information on continuous school improvement issues.
   (a) Background of information on requirements for continuous school improvement
   (b) ESSA and requirements for stakeholder participation in planning for continuous school improvement
   (c) Discussion of the types of data obtained in the SWOT analysis and the importance of the data to school leaders

Methodology used to conduct the SWOT and data analysis (third person) (15 points)

    (a) Discuss how the SWOT was conducted

    (b) Discuss the six factors included in the SWOT and why each is significant in terms of school improvement

    (c) Discuss methods used to analyze SWOT data

Findings (first person) (25 points)

Address the following questions in your findings:

    (a) Discuss three strengths found in your analysis of the information from the SWOT data.

    (b) Discuss three weaknesses found in your analysis of the information from the SWOT data.

    (c) Discuss why it is important to consider the role of the person providing information for the SWOT.

    (d) Was there any information obtained in the interviews that provided new, unknown information?

    (e) How might the information be best used by a school leader in planning for school improvement?

Implications for School Leaders (first person) (10 points)

As a school leader, how might you address the issues that surfaced in the SWOT analysis? At least **two well-developed** paragraphs are required.

References (APA format) (10 points)

A minimum of five references are required for the briefing paper and must be cited correctly in the paper and in the reference list. Refer to the APA guide in course resources to help you create the reference list.

Overall Paper Criteria (15 points). See criteria outlined.

CRITERIA	EXEMPLARY	PROFICIENT	DEVELOPING	UNACCEPTABLE
The required sections are included: 1. Introduction 2. Background Information and Literature Review 3. Methodology and Data Analysis 4. Findings 5. Implications for School Leaders 6. References	All sections are included and discussed thoroughly.	Most sections are included and discussed.	Sections are not included and there is little information in the sections.	The required sections and discussion are not included.

(Continued)

(Continued)

CRITERIA	EXEMPLARY	PROFICIENT	DEVELOPING	UNACCEPTABLE
Proper grammar, spelling, and sentence structure. **Hint:** *Spell and grammar check your work before submission.*	Excellence in grammar, spelling, and sentence structure. Sentences are not too long and are complete sentences.	Few errors in grammar, spelling, or sentence structure. Minor revisions needed.	Many errors in grammar and spelling. Appears that grammar and spell check were not used. Incomplete or run-on sentences throughout the work.	Work is difficult to comprehend because of grammar and spelling errors or there are many incomplete or run-on sentences.
Proper paragraph structure with a topic sentence and detailed sentences that flow directly from the topic sentence. **Hint:** *One sentence is never a paragraph in academic writing.*	All paragraphs have a topic sentence. Detailed sentences flesh out the information from the topic sentence in the order introduced in the topic sentence. End of paragraph leads into the next topic.	Nearly all paragraphs have a topic sentence and detailed sentences that flesh out the topic. Some paragraphs do not flesh out the topic in the order introduced in the topic sentence.	Many paragraphs lack a topic sentence, or the detailed sentences do not flow from the topic sentence. Detailed sentences do not follow the order introduced in the topic sentence. Work is hard to follow because of paragraph structure.	Paragraphs are hard to follow, and the writing does not flow because of the lack of structure.
Transition statements connecting paragraph to paragraph and section to section. **Hint:** *Headings are not transition statements.*	The writing flows from section to section and from paragraph to paragraph seamlessly with transition statements creating the flow. The reader experiences no interruption to the flow and understands how each concept or topic connects to the previous one.	Most of the writing uses transition statements well so the writing flows from section to section and paragraph to paragraph. There are some places where the reader doesn't understand how the previous concept or topic connects to the current one.	Much of the writing lacks transition statements, which connect one section to another or one paragraph to the next. The writing is choppy, and the reader doesn't understand how we got to the current topic or concept from the previous one.	Writing is very choppy. There are few to no transition statements to connect the ideas in the work.

CRITERIA	EXEMPLARY	PROFICIENT	DEVELOPING	UNACCEPTABLE
Citations to research articles throughout the work. **Hint:** *Citations can appear anywhere in a sentence, beginning, middle, or end, and can cite multiple works in a single set of parentheses.*	Research is cited appropriately throughout the work. Citations appear wherever they are appropriate, even midsentence.	Research is cited appropriately in the work, but there should be more citation of research. Citations appear wherever they are appropriate, even midsentence.	Research is not cited often, and citations appear only at the end of sentences or paragraphs. More citations are needed to support the writing, and/or citations should be made throughout the sentence.	There are few to no citations in the work, or the citations are done incorrectly so that it is not clear what work is being cited. Citations are only placed at the ends of sentences or paragraphs.
Citations and references follow APA formatting guidelines. **Hint:** *If any works are cited in the body of the paper, there MUST be a References list.*	Even at the exemplary level there may be some minor (easily corrected) errors in formatting. APA can be confusing. At this level the majority of formatting is correctly done per APA 7th edition.	Some minor (easily corrected) and a few major errors in formatting of citations and references occurred.	Major errors in formatting of citations and references seen such as use of MLA or Chicago style instead of APA formatting or a mix of various formatting styles.	Serious errors in APA formatting of citations and references present, or the citations or references are missing from the work.
Reference List: 1. Reference format: Each reference is cited in APA (American Psychological Association) format. 2. All references are listed alphabetically using the first author's last name. 3. A hanging indent is used. 4. Author(s), Date of article (year), Title of the article, *Name of the Peer-Reviewed Journal, volume*(issue), pagination, and digital object identifier (doi).	Referenced works are authoritative research articles that have an author(s). Each reference is cited in the paper. Each citation in the paper is listed in the reference list.	Nearly all referenced works are authoritative sources that have an author(s). Most references are cited in the paper. Nearly all citations in the paper are listed in the reference list.	Some of the referenced works have no author or are not from authoritative sources. Some references are cited in the paper; some citations are in the reference list.	There are few authoritative resources cited in the paper or reference list.

Formatting of the paper follows APA 7th edition guidelines, including 1-inch margins on all sides, double-spacing with no extra white space before or after headings or paragraphs, 12-point (Times New Roman) font. **Total Score: /100**

SWOT INTERVIEW OR SURVEY FORM

Add additional questions and room for responses as needed.

Interviewee #_____ Teacher ☐   Leader ☐   Community member ☐

SAMPLE QUESTION	RESPONSE
STRENGTHS	
What are possible advantages our school has over other schools in our district or surrounding districts?	
What does our school do better than any other school/system in this area?	
What do you think other schools see as our strengths?	
What does the public (community) see as our strongest points?	
WEAKNESSES	
What do we need to improve in order to be a better school?	
What are things (programs, issues) we should avoid?	
What do you think other schools see as our weaknesses?	
What factors could create turmoil in our school?	
What do you think the general public sees as our greatest weaknesses?	
OPPORTUNITIES	
What possibilities have the greatest potential to bring about positive changes for our school/community?	
What trends in the outside world could have a positive impact on our school?	
What external factors could have a positive impact on our school?	
What changes in state/local governance (elected officials/appointed officials) could have a positive impact on our school?	
THREATS	
What are the obstacles facing our school that could have the greatest negative impact?	
What are other schools doing that may have the greatest negative impact on our school?	
What state and/or local political factors could have a negative impact on our school?	

REFERENCES

Clardy, A. (2013). Strengths vs. strong position: Rethinking the nature of SWOT analysis. *Modern Management Science & Engineering, 1*(1), 100–123.

Ghazinoory, S., Abdi, M., & Azadegan-Mehr, M. (2011). SWOT methodology: A state-of-the-art review for the past, a framework for the future. *Journal of Business Economics and Management, 12*(1), 24–48.

Gurel, E., & Tat, M. (2017). SWOT analysis: A theoretical review. *Journal of International Social Research, 10*(51), 994-1006. doi: 10.17719/jisr.2017.1832

Pahl, N., & Richter, A. (2007). *SWOT analysis. Idea, methodology and a practical approach.* GRIN Verlag.

Pickton, D. W., & Wright, S. (1998). What's SWOT in strategic analysis? *Strategic Change, 7*(2), 101–109.

Saitis, C., & Saiti, A. (2018). The function of planning and programming. In C. Saitis & A. Saiti, *Initiation of educators into educational management secrets* (pp. 31–60). Springer.

Sarsby, A. (2016). *SWOT analysis.* Spectaris.

PESTLE Case Study

A case study in educational leadership provides a narrative that presents information to be considered by school leader candidates to represent multiple perspectives. Case studies offer background information about a subject from a school- or district-based context without offering outcomes.

Case studies are often problem based; this forces the school leader candidate to consider actions or decisions and to make recommendations. Case studies represent multiple school settings and situations that often cause challenges for school leaders because there are no clear right or wrong answers. Analysis and decision making become the responsibility of the school leader candidate.

PESTLE ANALYSIS CASE STUDY STUDENT LEARNING OUTCOMES

1. Students will utilize the information provided in the case study background information. School leader candidates will select processes to obtain information about potential school and district problems, recognize multiple internal and external influences and perspectives about education in the school and district, and apply problem-solving and decision-making processes such as those faced by school leaders.
2. Students will conduct a PESTLE analysis using the questions provided for the case study with a sample stakeholder committee.
3. Students will review the information obtained in PESTLE interviews and analysis of interview information from the perspective of a school leader.
4. Students will evaluate the information provided from the analysis and construct some generalizations about the information obtained.
5. Students will consider how the information obtained might apply to their own school or district.
6. Students will infer how the ideas, concepts, and perspectives generalize in a broader manner to other schools in the region.
7. Students will create a briefing paper using data obtained from the PESTLE case study background information.

PESTLE CASE STUDY BACKGROUND INFORMATION

WHAT'S A SUPERINTENDENT TO DO?

Dr. Tim Doroughty is the assistant superintendent of schools for research and development who was challenged to a new task by his new superintendent, Dr. Mariano Duggins. Dr. Duggins wants a PESTLE analysis of the school district following the COVID-19 pandemic and the turbulence of social unrest. Dr. Doroughty admits that he has never conducted nor participated in a PESTLE analysis and is open to learning, but he has several questions and concerns. On his way to a meeting with Dr. Duggins, he is busy reviewing his research on the purpose of the PESTLE and how to organize such an activity. What does he need to know?

What Is a PESTLE?

PESTLE stands for political, economic, sociocultural, technological, legal, and environmental. A PESTLE analysis is an analytical tool available to schools to determine how external factors influence their operations and how to make them more effective. PESTLE is a variation of PEST, which takes only the first four factors into account. PEST analysis (political, economic, social, and technological) is a method from which a school can assess major external factors that influence its operation in order to have more continuous school improvement. The PESTLE approach includes the additional aspects of legal and environmental issues that might affect a school (Sammut Bonnici & Galea, 2015). A PESTLE analysis is used to gauge external factors that could impact the effectiveness and efficiency of the school and is usually used in conjunction with SWOT analysis to provide a comprehensive view of the school operations and environment.

PESTLE analysis is an assessment of the external environment as well as an array of other factors that can influence not only the present but also the future undertakings of the school. Once external factors are identified, that is, technological, social, economic, as well as political factors, the school will be in a position to consider strategies that position the school to benefit from changes in these factors while at the same time ensuring that the changes do not impact negatively on the school (Burt et al., 2006). Political, economic, sociocultural, technological, ecological, and legal (PESTLE) factors need to be considered (Carpenter & Sanders, 2006). PESTLE factors are judged according to their expected impact, the probability that these trends will increase, and the perceived urgency for the school to address them.

What Are the Elements of a PESTLE Analysis?

A comprehensive assessment of the major areas of influence that affect the school, as well as the school itself, can contribute to a more comprehensive view of the environment in which the school operates. PESTLE assessments can be undertaken to maximize the school's ability to capitalize on conditions as they exist and to be forewarned of and better prepared for imminent changes or dangers in the environment.

The *political* aspect of PESTLE analysis focuses on the areas in which government policy and/or changes in legislation affect the educational system overall and the school in particular. The general political climate of a nation, state, region, or city can also greatly influence the school. A prime example is the current COVID-19 pandemic and its impact on public schools.

The *economic* portion of the analysis targets the key factors of economic growth or decline. Schools are dependent on funds delegated from the state and may receive additional revenues from local authorities. Swings in economic fortunes directly affect schools and the provision of faculty and staff and all other operational aspects of a school.

The *social* factors that may be included in a PEST analysis are demographics and age distribution, cultural attitudes, and workplace and lifestyle trends, sometimes labeled as *sociocultural* factors, which include family structures, education levels, and crime levels. Demographic factors include the socioeconomic makeup of the students attending a school and are intertwined with the economics of where the school is located.

The *technological* component considers the specific role and development of technologies within the school, as well as the wider uses, trends, and changes in technology. School district spending on technology may also be a point of interest in this area (Çitilci & Akbalık, 2020). Technology funding for schools is also derived from state and local school funding; lack of funding affects how much technology can be provided for students, access to technological resources such as internet infrastructure, and rapidly expanding requirements for e-learning or online learning.

The **legal** components are also connected to the economics and technological factors in a school. Schools must adhere to regulatory and accreditation factors required for operations. Federal and state regulations affect school finances, and changes in legislative measures also affect schools. Additionally, legal components such as safety compliances can be challenging factors for schools.

The *environmental* factors include both ecological and environmental aspects, which include whether the school buildings satisfactorily meet community needs. Physical factors, which include physical space appropriate to the age of students, lighting, temperature, and access to resources for abled and disabled persons, are important to ensure continuous school improvement. Additional factors include having enough classrooms to service student needs and safety and compliance factors.

Advantages of a PESTLE Analysis

PESTLE analysis can assist schools in recognizing opportunities offered by existing conditions in the environment. It can also be used for identifying current or possible future challenges to help school leaders plan for how to best manage these challenges. PESTLE analysis can also be applied in assessing the in-house structure of an organization to identify strengths and weaknesses in its internal politics, economic outlook, social climate, and technology base. The results of this analysis can facilitate changes or improvements in areas identified as needing attention, more resources, and continued development (Gupta, 2013).

PESTLE analysis can be used in conjunction with a SWOT analysis for comprehensive results. Conducting a comparison between completed analyses can provide a very solid basis for informed decision making. Data from the analyses can be applied to any segment of the school or to the total school environment. When a school leader uses PESTLE, it can identify ways to take better advantage of a situation of strength, overcome a situation of weakness, and avoid making mistakes in the educational and social environment (Diderich, 2020).

PESTLE analysis permits school leaders to examine factors when making decisions about the school's services to students and the community. One key factor may be demographics of the community, including growth or decline in community population or business and industrial demographics. These demographics are a direct reflection on the demographics of the school population. Changes in demographics predict changes in school populations. Changes in the education environment can create great opportunities for the school while simultaneously causing significant threats. For example, opportunities can come from new and emerging technologies to reach more students or teach them more effectively. Threats can include changing demographics that can alter the school organization.

Results from PESTLE analysis allow the school leader to make specific choices when planning the school's future, consideration of student numbers (increase or decrease) to staffing changes, technology needs, and the development of new programs or services (Bardach & Patashnik, 2020). PESTLE analysis helps school leaders understand the "big picture" forces of change to avoid threats and take advantage of the opportunities presented (Ho, 2014).

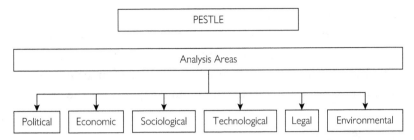

Figure B.1 PESTLE Analysis Elements

Procedures for Conducting a PESTLE Analysis

1. Designate a leader who has good group process skills and who can keep things moving.
2. Introduce the PESTLE analysis method and its purpose. This can be as simple as proposing, "As a starting point, let's consider the issues that schools are facing and make a list."
3. Depending on the nature of the group, have all participants introduce themselves. Then divide into smaller groups. If the meeting draws several groups of stakeholders together, make sure to mix the small groups to get a range of perspectives and give them a chance to introduce themselves. The size of these depends on the size of the entire group; breakout groups can range from three to 10. If the size gets much larger, some members may not participate.
4. Have each group designate a recorder and provide each with a device to record the discussion.
5. Give the groups 20–30 minutes to brainstorm and fill out the strengths, weakness, opportunities, and threats chart. Encourage participants not to rule out any ideas at this stage or the next.
6. Remind participants the way to have a good idea is to have lots of ideas. Refinement can come later. In this way, the PESTLE questions promote valuable discussion within groups.
7. Once a list has been generated, it helps to refine it to the best 10 or fewer points so that the analysis can be truly helpful.
8. Reconvene the group at an agreed-on time to share results. Gather information from the groups, recording in electronic format to collect and organize the differing groups' ideas and perceptions.
9. Proceed in PESTLE order, recording strengths first, weaknesses second, and so on.
10. Ask one group at a time to report.

11. Discuss and record the results.
12. Prepare a written summary of the PESTLE analysis to share with participants for continued use in planning and implementation.
13. The PESTLE process can be used with a variety of groups related to the school to collect valuable data and build support for the process.

Why Use a PESTLE Analysis?

School leaders need to be systematic and strategic in school improvement planning. External factors can impede the processes needed to improve student academic achievement through changes in political policies, economics, demographic changes, and access or lack of access to technology, and in our current world, changes in our environment that have affected students in terms of learning as schools have moved to different models of teaching.

Like SWOT analysis, PESTLE analysis identifies what exists, gaps, and areas need to be addressed for improvement. PESTLE and SWOT analyses allow school stakeholders to identify challenges and barriers to improving student achievement.

PESTLE and School Improvement Planning

PESTLE analysis as a part of the continuous school improvement planning process provides a two-part process to engage and query stakeholders to gain a broader perspective on issues affecting educational outcomes: identifying issues and then prioritizing the issues. With the persistence of student achievement gaps, SWOT and PESTLE analyses should be part of a needs assessment process as both in-school and out-of-school factors affect student academic achievement. Using SWOT and PESTLE brings a broader and more community-based approach for consideration and allows stakeholders to understand that broader issues have effects on education.

CONCLUSIONS

1. PESTLE is a realistic and reliable tool for use by school leaders for scanning the school and/or district environment.
2. PESTLE provides school leaders with a tool to assist with future prediction and analysis and brings broader issues affecting student achievement for consideration.
3. PESTLE is primarily used for assessing the environment external to the school, which ultimately affects students and academic achievement.

SCHOOL LEADER CANDIDATE ASSIGNMENTS

- Review the information in the background information.
- Assemble a mock stakeholder community to participate in a PESTLE analysis.
- Conduct the PESTLE analysis with stakeholders.
- Analyze the data from the PESTLE analysis.
- Assemble and present the findings from the PESTLE analysis.
- Prepare a briefing paper on the PESTLE analysis, processes, findings, and implications for school leaders.

Procedures to Complete Assignments

1. Review the information provided in the case study background information.
2. Reread the information in the chapter to evaluate the types of information needed in PESTLE analysis to construct a committee of stakeholders.
3. Establish a stakeholder committee. The stakeholder committee should be composed of a minimum of five and a maximum of 10 people. School leader candidates may consult with stakeholders through virtual mediums through interviews or surveys. Stakeholder representatives should include, if possible, three teachers, one school leader, one parent, and at least one community member. No committee member should be identified by any personal information.
4. Conduct a PESTLE analysis with the committee members to obtain information about potential school and/or district problems, recognize multiple internal and external influences and perspectives about education in the school and district, and apply problem-solving and decision-making processes such as those faced by school leaders.
5. Evaluate the information obtained in PESTLE interviews or surveys and analyze data obtained from the perspective of a school leader.
6. Assess the findings to construct some generalizations about the information obtained.
7. Predict how the information obtained might apply to a student's school or district.
8. Infer how the ideas, concepts, and perspectives generalize to other schools in the region.
9. Create a briefing paper using data obtained from the PESTLE case study background information.

PESTLE ANALYSIS BRIEFING PAPER RUBRIC

STUDENT'S NAME
Briefing Paper Rubric (Maximum of Eight Pages*) 100 Points

Write a short paper (five APA-style pages) based on the topic: PESTLE analysis.

There are six required sections in the briefing paper (Introduction, Background Information and Literature Review, Methodology and Data Analysis, Findings, Implications for School Leaders, References).

- Each should be labeled. Designated sections are to be written in third person.
- Two sections (Findings and Implications) can be written in first person as school leader candidates are addressing the issue from their base of knowledge.

Introduction (to the topic) (third person) (10 points)

Include discussion on the following questions in the introduction of the briefing paper:
(a) Introduce the topic
(b) Discuss the need for a school leader to obtain the information found in a PESTLE analysis

Background Information and Literature Review (third person) (15 points)

Five peer-reviewed journal articles, not less than 5 years old, should be used to provide supportive information on continuous school improvement issues.
(a) Background of information on requirements for continuous school improvement.
(b) ESSA and requirements for stakeholder participation in planning for continuous school improvement.
(c) Discussion of the types of data obtained in the PESTLE analysis and the importance of the data to school leaders.

Methodology used to conduct the PESTLE and data analysis (third person) (15 points)

(a) Discuss how the PESTLE analysis was conducted.
(b) Discuss the six factors included in the PESTLE and why each is significant in terms of school improvement.
(c) Discuss methods used to analyze PESTLE data.

Findings (first person) (25 points)

Address the following questions in your findings.
(a) Discuss three strengths found in your analysis of the information from the PESTLE data.
(b) Discuss three weaknesses found in your analysis of the information from the PESTLE data.
(c) Discuss why it is important to consider the role of the person providing information for the PESTLE.
(d) Was there any information obtained in the interviews that provided new, unknown information?
(e) How might the information be best used by a school leader in planning for school improvement?

Implications for School Leaders (first person) (10 points)

As a school leader, how might you address the issues that surfaced in the PESTLE analysis? At least **two well-developed** paragraphs are required.

References (APA format) (10 points)

A minimum of five references are required for the briefing paper and must be cited correctly in the paper and in the reference list. Refer to the APA guide in course resources to help you create the reference list.

Overall Paper Criteria (15 points). See criteria outlined below.

CRITERIA	EXEMPLARY	PROFICIENT	DEVELOPING	UNACCEPTABLE
The required sections are included: 1. Introduction 2. Background Information and Literature Review 3. Methodology and Data Analysis 4. Findings 5. Implications for School Leaders 6. References	All sections are included and discussed thoroughly.	Most sections are included and discussed.	Sections are not included and there is little information in the sections.	The required sections and discussion are not included.
Proper grammar, spelling, and sentence structure. **Hint:** *Spell and grammar check your work before submission.*	Excellence in grammar, spelling, and sentence structure. Sentences are not too long and are complete sentences.	Few errors in grammar, spelling, or sentence structure. Minor revisions needed.	Many errors in grammar and spelling. Appears that grammar and spell check were not used. Incomplete or run-on sentences throughout the work.	Work is difficult to comprehend because of grammar and spelling errors or there are many incomplete or run-on sentences.
Proper paragraph structure with a topic sentence and detailed sentences that flow directly from the topic sentence. **Hint:** *One sentence is never a paragraph in academic writing.*	All paragraphs have a topic sentence. Detailed sentences flesh out the information from the topic sentence in the order introduced in the topic sentence. End of paragraph leads into the next topic.	Nearly all paragraphs have a topic sentence and detailed sentences that flesh out the topic. Some paragraphs do not flesh out the topic in the order introduced in the topic sentence.	Many paragraphs lack a topic sentence, or the detailed sentences do not flow from the topic sentence. Detailed sentences do not follow the order introduced in the topic sentence. Work is hard to follow because of paragraph structure.	Paragraphs are hard to follow, and the writing does not flow because of the lack of structure.

(Continued)

(Continued)

CRITERIA	EXEMPLARY	PROFICIENT	DEVELOPING	UNACCEPTABLE
Transition statements connecting paragraph to paragraph and section to section. **Hint:** *Headings are not transition statements.*	The writing flows from section to section and from paragraph to paragraph seamlessly with transition statements creating the flow. The reader experiences no interruption to the flow and understands how each concept or topic connects to the previous one.	Most of the writing uses transition statements well so the writing flows from section to section and paragraph to paragraph. There are some places where the reader doesn't understand how the previous concept or topic connects to the current one.	Much of the writing lacks transition statements, which connect one section to another or one paragraph to the next. The writing is choppy, and the reader doesn't understand how we got to the current topic or concept from the previous one.	Writing is very choppy. There are few to no transition statements to connect the ideas in the work.
Citations to research articles throughout the work. **Hint:** *Citations can appear anywhere in a sentence, beginning, middle, or end, and can cite multiple works in a single set of parentheses.*	Research is cited appropriately throughout the work. Citations appear wherever they are appropriate, even midsentence.	Research is cited appropriately in the work, but there should be more citation of research. Citations appear wherever they are appropriate, even midsentence.	Research is not cited often, and citations appear only at the end of sentences or paragraphs. More citations are needed to support the writing and/or citations should be made throughout the sentence.	There are few to no citations in the work or the citations are done incorrectly so that it is not clear what work is being cited. Citations are only placed at the ends of sentences or paragraphs.
Citations and references follow APA formatting guidelines. **Hint:** *If any works are cited in the body of the paper, there MUST be a References list.*	Even at the exemplary level there may be some minor (easily corrected) errors in formatting. APA can be confusing. At this level the majority of formatting is correctly done per APA 7th edition.	Some minor (easily corrected) and a few major errors in formatting of citations and references occurred.	Major errors in formatting of citations and references seen such as use of MLA or Chicago style instead of APA formatting or a mix of various formatting styles.	Serious errors in APA formatting of citations and references present or the citations or references are missing from the work.

CRITERIA	EXEMPLARY	PROFICIENT	DEVELOPING	UNACCEPTABLE
Reference List: 1. Reference format: Each reference is cited in APA (American Psychological Association) format. 2. All references are listed alphabetically using the first author's last name. 3. A hanging indent is used. 4. Author(s), Date of article (year), Title of the article, *Name of the Peer-Reviewed Journal, volume* (issue), pagination, and digital object identifier (doi).	Referenced works are authoritative research articles that have an author(s). Each reference is cited in the paper. Each citation in the paper is listed in the reference list.	Nearly all referenced works are authoritative sources that have an author(s). Most references are cited in the paper. Nearly all citations in the paper are listed in the reference list.	Some of the referenced works have no author or are not from authoritative sources. Some references are cited in the paper; some citations are in the reference list.	There are few authoritative resources cited in the paper or reference list.

Formatting of the paper follows APA 7th edition guidelines, including 1-inch margins on all sides, double-spacing with no extra white space before or after headings or paragraphs, 12-point (Times New Roman) font. **Total Score: /100**

PESTLE INTERVIEW OR SURVEY FORM

Add additional questions and room for responses as needed.

Interviewee #_____   Teacher ☐   Leader ☐   Community Member ☐

SAMPLE QUESTIONS	RESPONSE
POLITICAL	
What possible political changes at the federal/state/local levels could have an impact on our school/system?	
When is the country's next local, state, or national election? How could this change government or regional policy?	
Could any pending legislation or taxation changes affect the school, either positively or negatively?	
Are there any other political factors that are likely to change?	

(Continued)

(Continued)

ECONOMIC	
How stable is the current economy, locally, regionally, statewide, and nationally? Is it growing, stagnating, or declining?	
Is the community income rising or falling?	
How is this likely to change in the next few years?	
What is the unemployment rate?	
How has the pandemic (or other disaster) affected the economic environment?	
Are there any other economic factors that should be considered?	

SOCIOLOGICAL	
What possible changes in the state's/community's attitude toward education could have an impact on our school/community?	
What social attitudes could impact the school? Have there been recent sociocultural changes that might affect this?	
How do religious beliefs and lifestyle choices affect the population?	
Are any other sociocultural factors likely to drive educational changes?	
What demographic changes/issues could have an impact on our school/system?	

TECHNOLOGICAL	
What technological challenges confronting our school/system today must be addressed?	
What emerging technologies have not yet had an impact on our school/system but are on the horizon?	
How have infrastructure changes affected work patterns (e.g., levels of remote working)?	
Should any other technological factors be considered?	

LEGAL	
What are the current legal challenges facing our school/system today?	
What potential legal challenges facing our school/system have not yet materialized?	
What current or future legal issues in the state/community could have an impact on our school/system?	

ENVIRONMENTAL	
What current environmental issues in the school/system could have an impact on our school/system?	
What environmental issues in the community/county have the potential to affect our school in the future?	

REFERENCES

Bardach, E., & Patashnik, E. M. (2020). *A practical guide for policy analysis* (6th ed.). CQ Press.

Burt, G., Wright, G., Bradfield, R., Cairns, G., & Van der Heijden, K. (2006). The role of scenario planning in exploring the environment in view of the limitations of PEST and its derivatives. *International Studies of Management & Organization, 36*(3), 50–76.

Carpenter, M. A., & Sanders, W. G. (2006). *Strategic management: A dynamic perspective, concepts and cases.* Prentice Hall.

Çitilci, T., & Akbalık, M. (2020). The importance of PESTEL analysis for environmental scanning process. In H. Dinçer & S. Yüksel (Eds.), *Handbook of research on decision-making techniques in financial marketing* (pp. 336–357). IGI Global. http://doi:10.4018/978-1-7998-2559-3.ch016

Diderich, C. (2020). Understanding the industry environment and its implications to strategy. In C. Diderich, *Design thinking for strategy* (pp. 79–92). Springer.

Gupta, A. (2013). Environment and pest analysis: An approach to external business environment. *International Journal of Modern Social Science, 2*(1), 34–43.

Ho, J. K.-K. (2014). Formulation of a systemic PEST analysis for strategic analysis. *European Academic Research, 2*(5), 6478–6492.

Sammut-Bonnici, T., & Galea, S. (2015). *PESTLE analysis.* Wiley.

Index

About the Authors

Pamela A. Lemoine, EdD, is an assistant professor in the Department of Leadership Development at Troy University, teaching and advising students in the masters and educational specialist programs. Dr. Lemoine is also the program coordinator for the global leadership doctoral program at Troy University. Dr. Lemoine completed a BA in English and an MA in educational technology and was awarded an EdD in educational leadership at the University of Louisiana at Lafayette in 2011.

Dr. Lemoine has over 30 years of experience in education serving as an elementary/middle school principal, district supervisor of elementary and middle school education, and director of federal programs before entering higher education. She has authored or edited books, published in professional journals, published numerous book chapters, and presented to state, regional, national, and international professional organizations. Dr. Lemoine's research interests include disruption and VUCA—volatility, uncertainty, complexity, and ambiguity—as well as educational leadership preparation and the impact of digital technology on education. Most recently, her interests have turned to the impact of the closures of educational institutions due to COVID-19 and how P12 and higher education institutions will face emerging challenges.

Delaine Dupree Bennett, EdD, served as a school administrator for 18 years before moving to higher education. She holds a faculty appointment as an assistant professor in the College of Education at Troy University, where she teaches instructional leadership and administration. She is also an active participant in youth leadership development and research projects within the Institute of Leadership Development at Troy University.

Dr. Bennett has a BA in early childhood education, master's degree in school psychometry and educational leadership from Troy, and an EdD from Columbus State University in leadership. As a school leader, Dr. Bennett served on numerous statewide school and academic councils as well as on statewide athletic committees. She has been an instructional leader in technology, differentiated instruction, and teen enrichment. Dr. Bennett has authored numerous articles related to strategic planning and leadership traits for today's leader as well as working on leadership in virtual schools. Dr. Bennett is currently working as a co-founder for a literacy program for young citizens.

Evan G. Mense, EdD, is currently a professor in the Department of Educational Leadership and Technology, which serves masters and doctoral students in educational leadership at Southeastern Louisiana University. Dr. Mense's research agenda is data-driven decision-making, and he has an extensive background in educational administration and leadership as a public school administrator.

Dr. Mense holds a doctorate in educational leadership from Saint Louis University, a master's of science degree in administration from Pittsburg State University, and a bachelor's of science degree in education from Missouri Southern State University.

Michael D. Richardson, EdD, is professor of educational leadership at the Global Tertiary Institute. He previously held faculty and administrative appointments at Columbus State University, Western Kentucky University, Clemson University, Georgia Southern University, Mercer University, and Southeastern Louisiana University. He completed a BS and an MA in education at Tennessee Technological University and was awarded an EdD in educational administration from the University of Tennessee. Dr. Richardson served as a secondary and elementary principal, personnel director, director of special projects, coordinator of federal programs, and assistant superintendent before entering higher education.

Dr. Richardson served as founding editor of the *Journal of School Leadership,* an internationally refereed journal of educational leadership, founding editor of *Contemporary Issues in Educational Leadership,* and editor of *The Journal of At-Risk Issues.* He has authored or edited 17 books, published more than 155 articles in professional journals, published more than 40 book chapters, and made more than 250 presentations to state, regional, national, and international professional organizations.

Dr. Richardson has chaired more than 85 dissertations and continues to actively and collaboratively conduct research and write for publication. His current research areas are organizational theory, particularly resiliency of leaders, phenomenology, and the implications of technology for administrators.

CPSIA information can be obtained
at www.ICGtesting.com
Printed in the USA
LVHW050433010422
714934LV00005B/381